GAUDY SORROW

by

Barbara Seyda

Finishing Line Press
Georgetown, Kentucky

GAUDY SORROW

Copyright © 2024 by Barbara Seyda
ISBN 979-8-88838-444-2 First Edition
All rights reserved under International and Pan-American Copyright Conventions. No part of this book may be reproduced in any manner whatsoever without written permission from the publisher, except in the case of brief quotations embodied in critical articles and reviews.

ACKNOWLEDGMENTS

To the indisputable muses: Kimi, Sydne, Shelly, Stephanie, Vicki, Elena, D.R. and Darrell. Thank you for pulling me out of the wreckage.

Deep gratitude to trans poet laureate T.C. Tolbert and *'Queer/Trans Space'*, a tuition-free, weekly poetry course offered by the University of Arizona during the entire global pandemic and it's aftermath. Relentless praise for my fellow students, seekers and scribes who knocked it out of the park every Wednesday at 4 pm via zoom. Thank you for your beauty, bravery and blood.

An exuberant bow to Leah Maines and Kevin Maines, publishers of Finishing Line Press. And my invaluable editor Christen Kincaid. And to Bill Risner, for generous, wise and incisive counsel.

For every battered poem pinned to the poetry clothesline in Broadmoor on the Treat St. walkway.

And the unnamed, anonymous, nocturnal Urban Poetry Pollinators who scrawl indiscriminately on concrete and asphalt in the night.

Publisher: Leah Huete de Maines
Editor: Christen Kincaid
Cover Art: Valerie Galloway, Instagram@valeriegallowayarts
Author Photo: A.T. Willett
Cover Design: Elizabeth Maines McCleavy

Order online: www.finishinglinepress.com
also available on amazon.com

Author inquiries and mail orders:
Finishing Line Press
PO Box 1626
Georgetown, Kentucky 40324
USA

*My friend/lover Zigor died on December 24, 2020 of Covid-19
and brain cancer.
He was airlifted and didn't make it to the hospital.
These are my letters to him.*

For the Covid tribe.

Dear Zigor,   January 3, 2021

I'm sewing a dress from silk parachutes. Made in internment camps. Worn by sixteen different brides. A baby dress. High neck pleats. Long sleeves. Gold filigree clasp. Fuck this. Let's elope. Go to Vegas man. In pink vinyl hot pants and eat doughnuts. Drink blood. Cradle our unborn child in glitter disco boots. I got it. Defeat and failure are exactly the same thing. They will not ruin me. My ex calls tonight and tells me you died. She's carrying your tongue in a ziplock. I'm hit with a stray bullet. How did you learn to die?

The sick bring you livestock. A goat or fat pig. Or luna moth odorous with licorice. Remember how we met? In 2002 I'm scheduled for a treatment at Providence Institute. Someone says there's a Basque guy who does traditional healing. I'm ostracized by my family for a confrontation with my father and filled with angst. After the fourth treatment I leave you a lamb. A bouquet of roses tied with linen. And my number. You call. *'Basia, either I keep giving you treatments or we see each other on the outside.'* Our first date is at the B-Line amidst scruffy tinkerbells and Volvo-driving, yuppie couple utopias. On the curb we kiss. Banished. Blazing. Veering into an embankment of dysmorphic, bone-crushing love.

I enter a silent crime scene. A Polish madonna and child hacked to pieces by a madman. I pick you up and carry you across a small, unnoticed war zone to the bathroom. You are throwing up and covered in shit. Half naked, wearing brown pants. I argue with the RN because she doesn't want me to wash you. It's Guernica. A wretched Cubist mosaic. Everyone is lying. Hysterical aides enter the room wearing sunglasses and a coat of rabbit skins chanting. *'There are worthy and unworthy victims.'* They wrap invisible, yellow police tape around you. The stink of silence and perfumed alibis everywhere. Now I'm riding in the ambulance with a driver shit-faced and hung over from Christmas Eve. How long can decedent remains stay in the morgue?

Our second date is at a cheap diner Orbitz on Broadway. We're sitting in a tacky, cantaloupe-colored, vintage-upholstered, curvy booth. Eating stupid, opalescent, ice cream banana splits. We have a spat. I can't remember about what. '*I mean do you really like chimichangas?*' You're pouting. Petulant. I'm wondering how you can flicker and fold in on yourself crammed in all this '50's western memorabilia. You pull me in. We make out in the parking lot.

Describe something from your room. Describe the emergency airlift pilot. What altitude was he flying at? Describe something you always have trouble with. Are you wearing a *txapella* and red sash? A chromatic, Ukrainian accordion player starts a GoFundMe page for you. Tell me how to survive the day. Can you define hypoxic injury in specific detail? Describe your process for waking up. Tell me how to breathe and worship god.

Our third date is at your aunt's house in Marana. You introduce me to your uncle, make popcorn and shove a movie in the VCR. We lay on the roof all night staring at stars. It smells like horses. You hit your forehead on a tree branch and it starts to bleed. At sunrise we're next to the bedroom where your dead aunt's ghost lives. She mediates the impervious, ultra-excessive, protracted lush sex. Your grand slam cock foraging. Sporadic and tight. You stand naked in *la tia's* room just to check out the ghost. The brightest thing. I'm not afraid of midgets or male witches.

Act 3 of '*Our Town*' bites. Dead characters sit in chairs. They have a fierce attachment to the living. Emily talks to her mother. Mrs. Webb doesn't hear her. She returns to the cemetery and they discuss the idiocy of living people. Oblivious and nonchalant. Are we trapped in Wilder's third act? Two blocks away a white husky's staring out the living room window of a red brick single story. The dog is flanked by ugly curtains and dingy, acrylic landscape paintings. I wonder if this is you staring from heaven through thick, non-reflective glass. At me encased in the incessant chaos of the world.

Our fourth date is Basque rabbit stew and anal sex. I drive my white Plymouth over to a house on 22nd Street where you're staying. You're throwing cherries into a pot on the stove. We start sucking rabbit meat off the bones and drinking wine. I end up on the floor. Face smashed down. You grab the olive oil and lacquer your cock. Fucking my ass barnyard animal style. I feel like a pig in a snakeskin thong. Butchered and unearthed.

Are you my Diogenes? Begging to be tossed over the city walls for rabid dogs to scavenge? Living in a barrel on the streets of Athens. The ultimate minimalist. An irascible character engulfed in extreme self-neglect, squalor, social withdrawal, compulsive hoarding and lack of shame. He plucked a chicken and brought it to Plato's Academy. Saying *'Behold! I've brought you a man.'* A featherless bi-ped. You were a cosmopolitan hound. A citizen of the world. Carrying a lamp in daytime. On the west side of Reid Park, a hawk gripping a frantic squirrel flies over me. It's a diabolical sign from the underworld.

Date number five. It's your birthday. You're a Gemini in wide, low-rider, black denim jeans hanging *chollo* style. A mesh tank top. Long, insane Rapunzel hair. We get 123 pieces of *unagi*, yellowtail, crazy dragon, volcano and lion king rolls from Izumi Bar. You bring home-brewed *sake*. We have a picnic in the park. I bake a four-layer, Bavarian chocolate cake lathered with whipped cream and cherries dunked in rum. It's a castle of pure decadence melting in the brutal southwest sun.

Is death an un-fleshed arrival? A privileged foxhunt! What if heaven is anti-climactic? A hoax. What if we all get juked? And when you die, you go nowhere? What if the creator is short with an unruly pompadour? A moody, insecure paranoiac. A slimy casting agent with blurred vision and a bad attitude? Sitting on a red alligator faux-leather couch. With an undertaker running behind schedule. Mired in mud. Screaming *'The fish stinks from the head down!'*

What if heaven is held together with cotter pins and trap doors, filled with dead bodies and ashtrays that need to be emptied? What if god is a maudlin little fuck? Or she's a spellbinding choreographer like Pina Bausch and we're thrown into avant-garde rehearsals for loneliness and kept under surveillance? What was god doing anyway for 4.5 billion years before humans appeared? Maybe death is a grotesque, little play where everyone is playing a vile, idealized version of themselves? Searching for an audience on earth.

Sometimes we just sit legs criss-crossed on the floor. Staring at each other. Making a terrible maelstrom of ridiculous faces for hours. You're a consummate actor with one eyebrow that went way up. We are penniless and largely unacknowledged. When you laugh your face cracks like a battlefield. Images of conflict on thousands of glass plate negatives breaking. You put your head in my lap twirling and sucking strands of your hair. We both know how to *schottische*.

Are you having martinis with Jesus? Are you target-shooting squirrels and plinking tin cans? Are you crouched in a soiled tuxedo awaiting metamorphosis in the steerage compartment of a celestial cargo ship? Will we arrive in ruby silk or torn up like refugees with pustules and gout? No smoke hole. No fire exits. No return. Birds, butterflies. Souls of women who died in childbirth. Dead poets. Fierce goddesses who carry the sun. Marigolds. Ritual offerings of food. Is there sexual perversity in heaven? Or is it a championship-caliber, 18-hole, high-end golf course with Pebble Beach players sitting around in coral-colored polo shirts drinking gin analyzing their next shot? What's up with this sick video efficacy of prayer shit?

Your father is a Viet Nam combat vet. In 2002 he's dead and you're a twenty-five-year-old punk healer. Couch-surfing in your car watching cartoons. Your insides are crushed. You're a full-time drunk. An Aristotelian peripatetic. Your car. A travelling circus dressing room. A sadistic no-privacy zone. I'm writing letters filled with self-pity and diaristic indulgence. Kindof like now. You're extinct and obscene. At regular intervals we film ourselves having super-8 guerilla-style, slacker gangster sex. Dude, what's up with moral turpitude?

My uncle Oscar's neighbor killed a pig with a pen knife. She—the sow—is cut to pieces. Sounds like the Colosseum. It must be love. The premise is solid. But the execution would be tough. Stop shoutin'. What's eatin' you? Don't talk. Don't move. I want to remember you as long as I can. Like cheesy memories decoupaged on a purse. Oh darlin' we're always saying good-bye. Funny-looking little monkeys we are. Our honeymoon storm is over. How do we pull this glamour out of a hat? Why are there five vacuum cleaners in the alley tonight? All I can think about is your exculpatory cock. An inimitable geisha with long, luxurious hair.

This is gross. Nineteen years ago I was eating your ass on seventeenth street in Armory Park. It was a hot rim job. But you weren't properly bathed. I got a serious dirty sanchez. A mouthful of chicken feathers, nails, broken glass and crusty pieces of shit. I should have stabbed you then. Is being dead like taking ecstasy? Maybe one day you'll cry.

Death is a racket. Is sex obsolete in the afterlife? Are you a mutilated mannequin ruined by love and life on earth? A coalition of bones. A notorious inurnment of unmet desire. Is your soul in a gloomy, soot-filled, vacant lot? Is a pantheon of uniformed cherubs in lard vats wailing? Are millions of long-nosed bats with tongue erections hanging upside-down on cave walls in elaborate homosexual orgies? Is god giving blowjobs?

You ask to meet me at Ike's on Speedway for coffee and tell me we can't see each any more. It's 2003. No reason. It's an emotional blur. I'm slurry-bombed. Spurned. I assume it's because I'm twenty years older than you. And you can't imagine how this can ever work. I try to explain. Men my age wear toupees, have six ex-wives, drive yellow mustangs and eat grapenuts. I go to therapy in a historic law building on 6th Ave. My appallingly short, Italian therapist is rotating on a physio ball eating a salami sandwich yelling '*That stupid man!*'

I see Ivona and her Polish sheepdog Cupcake in Himmel Park tonight. She makes dope leather bags that look like post-modern paintings and has a voice like Mick Jagger. Ivona's ex-husband won a bunch of Grammys and tried to choke her to death. She's yelling in a leopard fake fur jacket '*Lay that pistol down!*' She's from Rzeszow, near Czyzow where my maternal grandfather Kowalik lived. What are you going to do for the next 1.3 billion years? Go to T.J. Maxx?

You drive fast, careening into low-class, bizzle binges. After our first breakup you disappear. I kayak to Isla Tiburon and record stories with Seri elders. I attend P.J. and Malika's wedding. I'm a riled and iced-up starlet in a junkyard of mind-numbing pain. I'm eating myself alive. I remember the taste of your tongue fermented like sweet Japanese rice.

I hate going inside. I don't like telling you how I feel. I despise penumbras and psychedelic wings of light. I think we should eat the ashes of the dead with horseradish and beets. Like veggie burgers. Drain their blood. Watch the underworld without flashes, flood lights or blaring spots. Nothing happens. Bioluminescent souls do not appear at the Ice Capades. Still strung up to their misgivings. No uber-hot hockey players in orange, ruffled, starfish costumes chasing the Zamboni. There's no redemptive moment or degenerative plot. No epiphany. Or Hildegard von Bingen isorhythmic motet. Our bodies are not the leaves of god. We are political, torn, bandaged instruments of war.

You killed a man. I still have the prison letters. Dug them out of a cardboard box in the garage last night. The prosecuting attorney called and grilled me. I think he wanted me to testify against you. I refuse. I tell him you're an alcoholic. He's aggressive and doesn't back off. You hit a motorcyclist who wasn't wearing a helmet. He dies. And you're convicted of involuntary manslaughter. In 2003 you disappear for five years. No one knew where. Tina calls with your address. A federal facility in Yuma. You're in a high-security yard with killers.

My friend Lisa works as a P.T. with inmates in the New Mexico system. She says vehicular manslaughter is common. She's treating a twenty-one year old who hit a skateboarder. He wasn't drinking but left the scene. Got fifteen. She says prison is summer camp or a hell realm. I can smell five kinds of fear on you. Bouquets of loneliness. Like brown, crumpled bags.

Excerpts from prison letters. May 18, 2005. Yo swangsta. I smear menstrual blood over your photo. I wrangle with all of your dead ancestors. And climb to the stone circle in Punta Chueca. I stare at stars in Black Canyon along the Colorado River and crawl into a sauna cave. It's like sliding into the esophagus of a dinosaur. Breathing and slimey. I honestly don't know why I care about you. You are so obsessed with yourself but feel like my spirit brother. An ancient friend. I don't care that you're a carnival of ruin. Your spirit dark, jackhammered and random. Love is a vortex of chaos. A locked-up, staggering beast.

Prison letter. June 4, 2005. I pass three prisons on the way to Pappas School for homeless children in Phoenix. I wonder if you're held in any of these facilities. The Pappas bus driver picks up over 800 kids who couch-surf and live in parking lots and arroyos. There's a little kid Julio at the emergency shelter who has long, dark, curly hair and doesn't speak. He's three. One day he sat next to me on a wooden bench in the kitchen, where it smelled like fried chicken and dirty diapers. I offer him papers and paint and he chose the colors he wanted. He shakes his head up and down to let me know what he wants. The next week they shaved his head. He hated his new baldy. Then he and his mom left. He's fragile and lost like you. Slashed deer eyes and skinned alive.

Prison letter. June 7, 2005. Two guinea hens run down the barrio at five a.m. I stand on my head for three minutes, eat four pork sausages and *berenjenas rebozadas*. I talk to a guy in a gorilla suit who's unhappiness is leaking through his fly. I forgot to tell you about the film crew from Hiroshima I had dinner with last week. They were in Madagascar for a month and then came here with $40,000 cameras, field vests, light meters, comfortable shoes and little hats. They found a pygmy owl and nest of babies at Saguaro East. They photograph my feet and project them onto a giant atomic bomb.

Prison letter. June 21, 2005. Last night I skip yoga and go to stripper night at 'The Biz'. I just want to look at naked girls and forget about *asanas* and eternal happiness. Six girls from 'Tens' were performing. I drank pineapple juice and try to avoid billowing cigarette smoke and loitering stares of butch dykes. I went to the john and Emerald one of the dancers is in the stall next to me. I see a tampon wrapper float to the floor between Valentino Garavani Roman Stud black-patent-leather stilettos and red fishnet panties. We wash our hands together and she smiles. A cascade of blackberry curls, tight-laced vinyl corset and peach areolas.

Prison letter. June 25 2005. I wake up at 4:30 a.m. and the moon is still bright. Clouds like a petticoat. I watch stars move across the sky. A curtain opening onto an endless stage. Constellations appear as the faces of animals. Coyote, mouse and wolf. I'm sleeping in a bed of tiny, scarlet flowers sprouting from the Bear Wallow Creek forest floor. Blood spots in an alpine field of green. I'm surrounded by Indian paintbrush, Mexican hats and columbine.

Prison letter. June 29, 2005. I'm in Room 137 at the Pima County Courthouse wearing my juror badge. I rode my bike snaking down alleys in early morning light. In the hall are portraits of Superior Court judges and photographs of gnarled tree roots, a pair of ice skates, a plastic doll with no head and a wheelbarrow filled with dead chickens. Evette has dark red, auburn hair and glasses and announces on a microphone *'No shorts! No halter tops! No skateboards! No rubber shoes!'* I'm glad I left my rubber shoes at home. I'm sitting next to a guy who's a fire enthusiast. I'm reading *'Naked'* by David Sedaris and he's reading a book on the history of fire. Later I'm dismissed from the first case involving DUI charges. I raise my hand, proceed to the bench and tell the judge about your conviction. The defense attorney stares squarely at me and adjusts his tie.

Prison letter. August 28, 2005. Alexa and Rena are inseminating this weekend. The sperm donor was over yesterday and split. He's back today. My visit is squeezed in between ejaculations. It's complicated when two girls want to have a baby. You can have sperm shipped frozen via UPS. Put it on your Visa and a batch will land on your porch in a big, cardboard box. You can adopt a Chinese baby girl, solicit a donation from your girlfriend's brother, get knocked up by a male friend or ex, hire a surrogate mom or utilize *in vitro* fertilization technology. Actually, I don't want some guy jerking off into a jelly jar in my bathroom right now.

Prison letter. September 4, 2005. I'm doing a photo shoot for Circus Girl with Bridget, the burlesque acrobat from Zuzi. She writhes into the sheer, chiffon corset like a viper in a hibiscus blossom. Bridget's a 26-year old starlet who used to be married to a Pentecostal Christian, who told her she was wearing the wrong clothes to church and saying bad things. I think she's a Romanian Danish Jew enchantress. A big, fat cat wanders toward her from the neighbor's yard nestling between her thighs. I put the red fur *spodik* on her with hand-blown glass birds hovering in a bouncy polka.

In 2008 I'm back from Amsterdam renting a pink, brick bungalow on Santa Rita from an eighty-six year old, manic depressive Mormon lady who crawled away from the Church of Latter Day Saints in Cedar City when she was three. I'm living next to a T.O. graffiti artist, his Navajo girlfriend and their baby. Two years later, Melanie will be raped by her best friend's husband while the toddler is sleeping. Unexpectedly you show up on the porch. I haven't seen you in five years. I'm hit in the face with a suitcase. We love each other way too much.

You get spit out of prison slurred and raked. Flashy. Locked in and tenuous. I try to be your friend. We don't fit anywhere. We squabble, wrestle and re-define ourselves for the next thirteen years. I feed you *borscht* before I leave for TCC Music Hall where I'm working wardrobe for *'Legally Blonde'* dressing the principal men. Musical theatre is a high-financed, vulgar cartoon. Everyone is filled with moist synergy and delirious. Four albino chihuahuas wearing hot pink, rhinestone collars have their own dressing room. A sign on the door reads *'Do not disturb the canine actors!'* This makes you laugh so hard it hurts.

Dirty human miracle. Poor soul. Mysterious Basque madman. Master of fungi. Silly child. Serious spirit. Male model. Vampire love zombie. Sheep-castrator. Fandango dancer. Stuntman. Shepherd. Liar. Cheater. Ex con. Felon. Actor. Ass-fucker. I hurl into the night. Mother of pearl. Bright marigolds. Are you compressed clay? Are you the final slice of man angel cake? Are you the hand puppet giving a hand job? Are you the rubber, squishy devil giving me bruises? O aquarium of confetti, open for me. Slash the piñata. Drag me through broken skulls. I've got all you need.

Sometimes you tell me prison stories. You made fried rice in a wok on bed springs. And got buckshot from indecent blowjobs with female guards. I don't know if anyone grabbed your dick in the yard. You don't do drugs and stay clean to avoid getting killed. That's all I know. You've been cast in Alejandro Gonzalez Inarritu's new film in New Zealand. It's exciting but you lose the gig due to New Zealand's no felon policy. We talk almost every day. Sometimes not for stretches.

Some smart ass should option the rights to your life story. You could be the new Don Draper. HBO or Netflix could do a post-Covid, post-traumatic stress, limited mini-series. It would outsell and surpass *'The Queen's Gambit.'* You also were a fucked-up, beautiful, child prodigy addict slaying the Russians.

I dye my hair cerulean blue. I'm flossing my teeth with trumpet vines. I see baby leopards and wild little animals. I'm seeking comfort in all the wrong things. I dated the devil. Were you an official five-star stud? You had a real wife and three kids and me in a ten-foot, sheer mylar, cut-out party dress. Oh brother. It's in the Akashic records. Does god have a nice voice? A cheap donkey will eat too much straw. Gold, women and linen should be chosen by daylight.

Lily on Facebook says there will be no memorial due to your numerous lovers, one night stands and domestic partner. That your family in Bisbee doesn't want anything to do with all those ratchety women. Lily met you on a film set. She played a weird cougar in a bar. You were a muscleman. Rock star. Gangster. Six foot two inches. One hundred and ninety-one pounds. Olive skin. Ethnicity other. I wish I was a turtle dove. Demented cougar says hey what's up.

In 2010 I get you a gig with Konstantina who wants a male model in a bathtub eating gingersnaps with a handsome, black bulldog named Julian. Konstantina is a high-end, Greek jewelry designer who was married to a brutal, Mexican drug lord. Until the day she leapt out of his car and smelted her jewelry stash into a gold couture line, banged and hammered by Hungarian goldsmiths. I measure your neck, 16 ½ inches, sleeve 37 inches and chest 43 inches. You like the idea of being covered in diamonds and rubies in a luminous pool of green light. Her custom grand-baroque, pearl-drop pieces are gobbled by Hawaiian heiresses and go straight into a vault. It's like locking up the Mona Lisa in a garage.

You're a joke. I gave birth to a magician. We drank Tamaulipas *mezcal* with a lot of complexity. Subtle pepper and cinnamon. I retrace the biography of your body. We're embroidering our faces with this loose, episodic structure and strange mood. Have you ever seen rain? Do you think when Adam sent Eve into a face plant it was a freakin' accident? Here in the pink twilight of my grief sits a mockingbird. Mocking me.

I send an email to your wife asking where you're buried. Your Slavic Mail Order Bride sends two nasty emails. *'I know who you are. I was warned!'* She's losing her grip. Says I'm cashing in on my pain. And that kings often obtain their disreputable women from backstage, illegitimate theatre. I erect an expandable, artificial ivy, faux-privacy fence around my repulsive heart. It costs five-hundred-thousand dollars to train German shepherds and hire a full-time *choomba*. Mail Order Bride says I'm a mistress. A sex slave and smokeshow. Evil mate poacher. Keep my grubby toes off your grave. It's so easy to go berserk. Do you think buying something at Walmart is utter sin? It's actually in the Old Testament.

I like to blow shit up. You hypnotic bird of paradise. Three-legged barking dogs are trapped in the radio. A prima donna rips her cum shot. Handprints of time and spiritual knowledge are everywhere. Are you the bloody effigy on my wall? Yesterday Zee met a black dude in the barrio. He asked her over to watch a DVD. He made greasy hamburgers and they fucked. She insists on fetishistic, non-binary, non-hetero-normative relationships. It's over now. The hamburger bro man escapade. Have you ever hooked up with someone you met in a driveway?

I have a meeting with Oprah's development exec today. She says they only want frothy tales. I don't even know what that is. Young, hungry screenwriters are willing to work for free. I'm in no rush. I'm like a Gila monster waddling out of hibernation. Remember when you got a buzz cut in lockdown? For a human hair donation? They sent you a polaroid of five, tiny kids with cancer who got wigs made of your curly, gypsy, black hair. A bunch of Basque, spunky, orphan Annie's scotch-taped to your cell wall.

I celebrate the broken. I'm eating shredded sentences and convoluted grief. You're the gorgeous view. Unintelligible. Infinite and tinted. I build a new anarchy boat. A Noah's Ark for exiled and renegade emotions. A little boy in a beret and short pants carrying a loaf of bread appears in my dream. My ninety-four year old aunt gets Covid. My uncle dies. Ellen Melamed who founded Jewish Lesbian Daughters of Holocaust Survivors dies. Michelle's boyfriend dies. Kristi's Big Mama dies. I'm watching another white, lesbian, 19th century pioneer drama on Hulu. My aunts are playing bingo and getting their hair done.

I call the Marana landfill today to see if your mother still works there. No one knows. No one cares. Dear rank stranger, you don't need to throw four hundred and eighty-nine gems in the local dump. Everybody's jealous. I'm sick of dark nights of the soul. Are you trying on different versions of forgiveness? What's up with the electric chemistry of shame and trauma bonds? I take clothes off the rack at dusk. The sky, orchid canker sore. I get extremely still and feel a deep, quiet belief that you're far away and never coming back.

You're an extra on a film shoot with Agnieszka Holland about a famous outlaw prowling the Slovak-Polish border. The script is by Eva Borusevicova. In 2010 you start signing all your emails *'Janosik'*. I'm jealous because you're in Poland working with a legendary, female director. I'm climbing Mint Spring Trail. Dead trees, blue beetles, sunflowers, fern and caterpillars engaged in a tenacious butoh rave. An inchworm plummets out of the sky and lands on my heart. What do you think *that* means?

I'm opposed to impressionism. I hate the sound of German. Even Schubert or Wagner or Mahler. It makes me sick and I feel like throwing up. A meth girl hangs out in the culvert and crosses Broadway with me. My eastern slav, inner thug comes out when faced with a slut hustler *kurwa*. This situation is so fucked from every angle. I'm still reeling from being sliced by your Rusnak Trans-Carpathian widow. Just for asking where you're buried. I got muscled out of queerdom. Are you treading water in purgatory? And saying glossy rosary sonatas?

In 2012 I'm airbrushing thirteen devil and demon leotards for Carmina Burana, the ballet cantata by Carl Orff. I'm hand-painting silk for the witches. And a seventeen-foot velvet cape on the floor of the U.A. dance studio. Jeremy, the misogynist, gay costume designer is getting my finest work. I have a bad dream about dismembering a wolf. You tell me a Turkish, tribal myth about a boy mating with a blue wolf. They have a cub. Half-human and half-wolf boy. This is the ancient she-god who separates earth from sky. You're unreal with dreams and curses. You remind me not to rely on you for happiness.

A few weeks later, you jackknife into the Pacific Ocean and swim with a whale for a Maori film shoot. I thought you were unbreakable, but you arrive suddenly and lay in my bed with several cracked ribs. You're vulnerable in public for the first time. You spew algorithms, multiple languages, obscure texts and recite Macbeth. You're a private bomb with a heart.

I have a psychic reading at 1 p.m. Lyssa does meat-and-potatoes bucket dreams and channels the dead. In 2015 she was possessed by the devil while living in New Orleans. And got a drive-by exorcism from a Toltec shaman. She says I'm super-human and you're an asshole. That I healed you. I'm a pro Hall of Fame, gold jacket-caliber, Vince Lombardi trophy-winning quarterback throwing gaudy sorrow and shade. But you got all the glory and manipulated me. I'm mad at myself. Not you. I left it all on the field. I have seven more months of this shit. We've had seventeen thousand lifetimes together. I'm doomed. This is dreadfully long. It's connected to patriarchal power and male privilege in nefarious and insidious ways. She says I'm stuck in one of my bitchy plays. Whatever.

I don't know who I am in this story. The psychic thinks you're a secondary character or a tick on my cat. I don't even have a cat. You're not important. I was duped. I'm supposed to smoke some killer weed and have mediocre sex later this year. I am not a psycho bulldagger full of remorse and regret. I've been spiritually ransacked. I'm taking this piece back. Yanking my shit out. I'm a one-eyed giant who can outwit humans and carve tombstones. Lyssa said to watch stupid t.v., pet a rabbit and pray to Our Lady of Czestochowa.

I go to the Slavic Festival with a quixotic Belarusian milliner from the opera. We're eating a *kielbasa* combo platter in 2013. I'm showing her photos of you doing the Polish axe dance. Lajkonik has all their new costumes laid out in the church hall. The Belarusian and I run our fingers over the ornate embroidery, tassels and lace. We're having an ecstatic experience. You're not there. But you are. You're on a film set in Sri Lanka making a micro budget, low-grossing movie that we'll never see.

The guy across the street hired a cavalcade of under-age, global pandemic hookers. No one wears a mask. They chain-smoke and at times a she-devil in a sequin halter will sweep the porch. My other neighbor is obsessed with keeping his lawn emerald green. In the main house, a straight Republican couple had a baby. No sweat. All these Covid babies. I adore her. The baby gave me the finger in the garage. I think she wonders why the world is so fucked.

Why does everyone worship Arthur Miller? I hope I'm not beefing with you at ninety-seven. The nursing home aide on duty will say oh she's fine. She's just ranting at the Basque who died thirty-five years ago. No good bye. No final note. No last conversation. No embrace. My favorite scene in Federico Fellini's '8 ½' is when Marcello Mastroianni's in a Roman bath house with his wife, mistress, sex workers and female journalist. They are powdering and primping him. Then a rejected showgirl starts a rebellion. Pandemonium ensues. Marcello grabs a whip and the place goes to hell. It's worth re-creating in some type of neo-expressionist, cathartic 21st century performance. Am I boring you?

I can't believe how many skanky B-movies you made. What about when you took off for Palm Springs to play a three-hundred-year old vampire with obligatory make-out skills? In the cult hit *'The Vampire and the Rabbi?'* The tagline was 'immortality sucks'. I'm done with mushy flashbacks and gazing into the past.

Your family is wackadoodle. So is mine. Secretive, superstitious, stubborn and paranoid. Maybe that's why we clicked. And then we didn't. Remember when we went to the Red Garter and did shots? Where are we going? I'm sick of puking. Joan of Arc was my first jerk off fantasy. Well, not really. It was actually the Sisters of St. Joseph. I kept a shoebox of nuns under the bed and would tear off their habits. Have you met Stalin or Charlie Manson or Fats Waller? Did you know Jeffrey Dahmer was murdered while cleaning the prison bathroom?

I climb Atascosa Peak. Feels like landing on the moon. Switchbacks through manzanita and scrub oak. I sit on the ground and pray. I eat pastrami on a bagel in Edward Abbey's old lookout tower. He was a fire spotter in 1968. You can see the big aching tooth of Baboquivari, Pena Blanca lake and Ruby. Endless light on folds in the earth. Are you unfazed about cruel, unconsummated love? Today a woman sees a fatal stabbing of two people on Zoom. Am I harboring bitterness?

What about bisexuals with quivering, black eyes on the edge of a bed? From three-foot lines of coke on a broken mirror. A sex opera taxidermy for the '80's. Or Lola Flash's infared girls sixty-nining like zebras in heat. Or do you prefer Artemisia Gentileschi's self-portrait as a female martyr in 1615? Or Judith slaying Holofernes with blood spurting from his neck dripping on bright, white bed sheets. I am not the butt of one long, historical, dirty art joke. Why don't I have a single photo of you? I will take a daguerreotype of my heart, crotch, moon and hands. Bruised light. Auric halo on a polished, silver plate.

You take me to meet your mom and sister. They're not home so we cruise through Marana belting Joan Jett's *'Drummer Boy'*. Joan's a female messiah disguised as a hardcore, rocker chick. You sing in velvet breeches hemorrhaging plastic memories from your hair. Kissing you is like cutting my hand. Blessed is the animal we built. Hideous nights devouring time.

I have a second reading with another psychic named Cassiopeia. She says I need to revise my relationship with the dead. She corkscrews into the bardo. A treacherous descent on a crystal lattice into seven archetypal levels of human consciousness. She says you're in crisis. And that I'm in soul dialogue with you. I need to breathe emerald and amethyst light. And welcome the rage. Because you bailed. In life and in death. My great-grandmother Katarzyna Budnyk Owczarzak is running a rad vengeance show. You're getting slimed.

My heart is hairy. Unkept. A smelly stud. A diabolical manhole. Fucking psycho. You are a calligraphy of Chihuly glass ceilings. A stage of sizzling idiots and chewed-up piano legs. I am blaming. Bat-shit crazy. A creepy, little bastard. Who won't shut the fuck up. I'm a garish venus in fur. Blown here by a cataclysm in sequin, over-the-knee boots that stretch clear to the crotch. Will you hold my parasitic heart? And it's big ass, holy macaroni love? And entire malicious and messy plot. I'm amazed at how oblivious love is. How it dies of unknown causes. Like a corrupt playboy watching bad t.v.

We cancelled my dad's 90th birthday party. He's been in pandemic lockdown for over a year. I hired a Dixieland band and polka band. We were going to make two-thousand mushroom and meat *pierogi*. I just sent him a book on Bob Hope. I also sent him a book on Cary Grant's bisexuality. I told him I'm writing a book about you. He asks if it's about how precious life is. I don't know how to answer that. I'm de-constructing the sonnet, *haibun* and *ghazal*. Seems like this whole town is insane.

I'm a rude hooligan. A plague poet. Guess it started with Boccaccio. Nobody cares about an ironic blowjob or if you evolve. When I remember you, I remember toe-sucking and the bloody tyrant. Your hand-painted counterfeit face. A hematoma on moldy bread. An imperfect actor. A decaying angel with real yak hair. I remember your wound and try to mouth hope. Heinous crime. Are you dialed in? Do the dead watch you masturbate?

I haven't been hugged in a year and a half. Last time was on the F-train platform in Brooklyn. My friend Titus and I were coming back from Will Eno's dissastisfying play *'Gnit'* at TFANA. You were a two-year-old insomniac. Wandering around the house at night. Can I be grateful for your offenses? Can I forgive your crimes? Can I accept your death? Am I still in love with danger and pleasure? Did I waste my time on a scumbag? Can I consecrate my sorrow? Hey you. King of slick, how does it feel to be dead?

I remember the lies. Your hit-man, porn star, gilded alabaster body. My romantic, kryptonite jewel heart. Nobody knows the entire tangled and contaminated story. You're being played as the world heaves it's bloody mantle. Beast and bloody spur. The unfinished symphony of scandalous feelings. And unwillingness to forgive. Today I burn frankincense and myrrh. Rattle my house to rid it of wretched tears. And the majestic, rustic sphynx moth. Your crazy, Rusnak, Trans-Carpathian widow has no jurisdiction over grief. All men are bad. And in their bad-ass-ness reign.

You fat face, ape-shit, vandal baby. Ectoplasmic feat. Glimmering astronomy. Distressed primrose. This magic thing you are squinting at is a giant sequin in the sky. Me. Split. Exposed. A brand new disaster of original sin. A hand-held, out-of-focus, smash-cut grainy sequence shot from behind. I am not a turnip. I'm a Polish witch. Your Slavic *montanka* doll. An effervescent sonogram of sorrow. Gutter mouth. Or blabber mouth. Sucking on bones of the alphabet. You and I are gliding inside a Samsung, eight-inch tablet of amniotic fluid and time.

I tear into the moment. Again. Death is an evacuated city. Filled with exotic birds and amber lips. Pigeons and wind. Wild turkeys. Honking snow geese. Coyote and quail. I do a saran wrap ceremony. I bend chicken wire, torn rage, and knotted, rusty metal onto your crown. I see you downstage surrounded by a multitude of colorful, Art Deco, terra-cotta ornaments. You shoot your wad into the audience. A saint performing a miracle. Five hundred people in Albuquerque groan in excitement. And horror. You, a *cazimi* landing in a dream.

Weird Cougar in a Bar says you private-messaged her and told her you have brain cancer. *'I didn't know this man!'* Cougar and I are going to meet for a dirty chai at Caffe Luce but she has a house fire and a tooth abscess. And she's afraid of Covid. So we chat on the phone. She's into quantum physics and Mahayana Buddhism. Says there's no separation when we transition. It's an extension. You're still part of everything. She remembers the cured olives you fed her.

Did you open your fly, grab the boa constrictor and thrust it into space one last time? A torn blessing. Flapping its wings of desire. And misery. The room without you is hollow, filled with emptiness and cuntilicious, plum-colored light. I walk into the parking garage, through long shadows of city busses, spray-painted with urban, splashy, commercial graphics, past pomegranate trees, corrugated metal mailboxes, trellises with no vines, devout women with expensive, satin hats and prayer books, *panaderias* and the menacing hooded face of god.

You're a huge, grey mass of nothingness. Your dressing room, a cinder block box of chartreuse light. You had a rolodex of phantom and real sex partners. I flipped through them like taking erotic confetti out of a box. You wander, a somnambulist through a divine, delirious nightmare. I feel deprived and rejected. You worry and want to yell as if chased by a shark. I'm ready for straps on a shoe. A pelvis. Eyelashes. A rampage. Or a tableau of small, undulating, brightly-lit, female body parts and a butterscotch, blinking anus.

I bury Covid Baby at the base of a giant eucalyptus. Burn copal at sunrise. Throw melon rinds and corn. Do you remember Esmerelda my desert tortoise? Who saw everything. Her elephant-skin face covered in magenta, prickly pear juice. She is the only witness. I make you a blanket of rabbit fur. Dead pigeon wings and Tarahumara squash seeds. I eat fried pork chops and mashed potatoes. Are you a primordial giant? A cyclops with one roving eye and outstretched arms? Breathing quietly. Grinding your teeth to a mangled beat.

I'm building a 70-foot drop for the ballet and working *'Guys & Dolls'*. In 2014, you're depressed and yelling in your sleep. I'm making savory pots of stew and paying attention to the wind. You're drawing ships that look like Renaissance old masters. You don't know where I live anymore. *'Beneath the pavement are shells, bones and silence.'* You're trying to be a better friend and then leave for Mongolia. A female desert tortoise can retain sperm for fifteen years after mating one time.

We're bickering about Virginia Woolf who you insist had a keen grasp of the obvious. I have two tickets for Brecht's *'Mother Courage'* but you're leaving for Istanbul. I'm sick of your line of *sucias* and that we've never had sustained intimacy. I'm camping in Death Valley and am principal dresser for the Wizard of Oz. *'You're like a spoiled little girl stuck in a man's body.'*

We write each other porn. Yours involves psychological swerves, split shanks, sadism and different kinds of Latin. You call me *'Maitasuna'* or beloved. Because my smut style is like Jack Kerouac on steroids, you're pissed about the ending to one my stories and quit speaking to me for three months. It's erotic fiction. It says so much. You slump around the room like Anais Nin's anonymous patron. And blurt, *'I'm not interested in the earth stabbing the sun.'* My favorite aphrodisiac is fate. Here's one for the cookie jar.

Under a hardcore, cast iron sky you begin writing to me in Polish. In 2016 my mom almost dies on Christmas Day and I can't be around you when you're hungover or hammered. We both read *'The Emancipated Spectator'* by Jacques Ranciere which you can't believe is written by a Frenchman. I'm in NYC for the snow-apocalypse, the second largest snowfall in the history of the big apple.

Fields of chamisa and sunflowers swirl upward. My Sophia Loren look-alike, kachina doll ex meets me for a chile burrito. We drive past fake dinosaurs, *ocotillo*, windmills and propane tanks. Caves spewing stalactites. Ridges cut with catsclaw and rabbit brush. Billboards with vintage lettering. Ochre adobe church walls straining to scrape the sky. Hatch chile pickers load a bus caked in dirt. I constructed you from desire and 1970's television. I'm Peggy Lipton and you're a 1957 re-run of *Zorro*.

Sophia Loren and I grab two frito pies and drive to Rio Arriba on your birthday. I march solemnly through the carved, wooden doors of El Santuario de Chimayo, built in 1816 on Tewa land. A small room, *el pocito* contains a round pit. I smear holy dirt on my heart while listening to the rocking prayers of other mourners, *vatos* and tourists. I gawk at a wall of *milagros* as evidence of the divine. Thousands of crutches, discarded canes, braces and wheelchairs fill the main chapel. El Nino de Atocha's *viga* ceiling is loaded with little shoes, clothing and photos of children who have died. Painted birds and vibrant flowers cover the three-foot adobe walls.

You're ludicrous. A mirage. Arrogant. Magnetic. Lost wandering down a long, unknown road with yourself. I was mesmerized by your fragmentation and pain. Raw and saturated razzle-dazzle. Understated allure and despair. I sent you curated, wide-angle shots of ocean waves, a child's shoes abandoned at Auschwitz and my ninety-five-year-old aunt who opens cans and exercises every day.

In dreamy, Andrei Tarkovsky-esque style I see your pink lips eating regret. Peeling an orange in a boxcar. You are soft and look like god. Did I give the gold envelope to the wrong man? I am trying to escape the wrath. Gagging. What's up with the foolish, rubbery grin? The carnival contortionists are smirking. The Russian guy has hummingbird teeth. And a bowl of *borscht*. An agenda. An old poem. Are you saluting the Basque flag? Printed on 3 x 5 heavy-duty polyester, available on Amazon with brass grommets. What are the noises of war? You and your fucking *pendejo* hook-ups. I will not be silenced by insidious fiends or circus of the shallow.

I despise Valentine's Day. I'm far more complicated than you think. Did the ambulance leave blood stains on the door? You're the only straight guy I know who's oblivious to pussy. And the historical significance of the vagina. Are you an incurable curse? I have lipstick, a chocolate sea monster, indigo Revlon mascara and metal tweezers. Your voice sounded like lava, footsteps, a baby crying and forgiveness. You, an unnamed constellation of stars. A private, erotic, meaningless cyclorama.

You come from a long line of giddy knife-throwers. Shaw said the more things a man's ashamed of, the more respectable he is. Well, that Jack Tanner. Against this swath of human canvas, you will not have a *gauela* procession led by children and young men carrying torches. Or funeral mass in *Euskara*. No incense, trumpets, minyan, *kaddish*, pyre or polka band with fermented, potato peel vodka. I met you when you learned *sendatzeko* from your *grandpere* Pempo. Once you sat on my bed and cried. I was playing a *jota* in C minor. You plunged into deep goblet squats, kicks and hurled an axe. An insane dance. I'm blind-sighted by Godzilla.

I go to In-N-Out Burger at El Con. I see Bronson who does pull-ups at the bus stop and used to flip kilos over the border. It's Wim Wender's slow motion, cinematic heaven. Ravenous people wait for double cheeseburgers and animal-style fries. Everyone looks like a 17th century masked cherub. Chubby babies painted by Peter Paul Rubens. Ripped Filipino homeboys heavily tatted. Sulking with cellphones and hands on their junk. Black ladies in mink coats and cha cha heels. Mormon families devouring strawberry shakes. South Asian girls in layers of cashmere and kabuki makeup. And drooling toddlers that could lacerate your face.

At lunch vultures fill the house. Oprah interviews Smokey Robinson on a flat screen, wall-mounted t.v. The Polish saint eats two breaded shrimp. Chicken noodle soup. Cranberry juice and a bowl of canned pineapple. I wear a turquoise, plastic, floor-length hospital gown, gloves and a mask so I don't contaminate the entire facility with a flesh-eating, fatal virus. I'm embedded in a bad, sci-fi, horror flick afraid to touch myself. My eyes roll up. I don't speak. Are you dying? I can feel your bones inside my skin.

I call your cell at 3:17 am just to hear your voice. I need a *relicario*. Some remnant of you. Like a pilgrim caught in an act of extreme devotion. I stare at the wall. A *penitente* experiencing an ecstatic vision. You sound like a thousand sandhill cranes. Migrating for the winter. Guttural and primordial.

A technician attaches twenty-two gold electrodes to your skull. Can I sit next to you and sing the *koledy*? Are you buried under a pile of clothes? Did you fall into a seam in the earth? You aren't allowed to drink wine or order in. Can I collapse into your rotting, rollercoaster skin? This is a malicious, petty, vengeful sideshow. You loved my feet and called me *Basia*. My body is sickened by secrets. I don't know if I still believe in a reckoning with god. Go back to the lowlands. He's dead. Play the Morbidoni midget, pearl squeezebox for him.

I'm shattered. In a fast-food, plastic booth with two small, pleated-paper containers of ketchup. Feeling my endangered heart. Poached. Breathing. Slimy. Furred. With a marsupial pouch and long tail. My heart, a mouth of serrated teeth. A tongue baked in an oven. A feral rat. Our umbilical cord runs through neon streets and upscale cravings. Dead-beat casinos, faux-swank hotels and vibrating palm trees. Erotic asphyxiation and all-you-can-eat buffets. Cries. Longs to return home. To the flowering earth. To eat cabbage. I whisper to you and grieve the unknown.

Shall I tie you to a chair with a rope? Torture a confession out of you. Like a true fem slam-dunk dominatrix. The catastrophe of you. Who cares? I'm eating gluten-free, jalapeno cheese puffs. Surviving the pandemic is all about soft home-décor and snacks. Black birds are screeching in the dead of night. Are you waiting for this moment to arrive? When are we going to laugh? At 2:48 p.m. eastern standard time, the moon will rise coughing up worms. If you're single, it's advisable to spend time with anyone who's not right for you. Just to take the edge off loneliness. Is god cranked up on power and cutting evanescent farts? What a snitch hipster. It's hard to say anything here without cringing.

Covid Baby has risen from the dead. She morphs into a very attractive, lethal virus with multiple variants and personalities. She's groovin' to *'Boogie Wonderland'* and Jimi Hendrix. She's decked in a muskrat fur onesie sucking a bright, green pacifier. Lately she struts down the alley *ala* Rick James. Checking out my anti-bodies. And teething. What the heck happened to all your baby teeth? Slavic Mail Order Bride is still shocked you led a double life. Get over it. Some men aren't meant to stay home and mow the lawn.

I'm fractured and murky. In a remote prison gutted of devotion and faith. Is this a trauma narrative? Am I an atrocity tourist? Dissecting my own heart. Can we interrogate tenderness? Can we be unscrupulous about love? I cover my body with nude kneaded erasers. I pull bloody scrolls out of my cooch. I drive through L.A. with a megaphone clamped to the top of a stolen Volkswagen bug. Blasting a non-stop, transient, grief monologue to oily, muscle men and surfers on Venice Beach. Am I your favorite, low-income, bisexual anti-hero?

I bike to El Rio Health on the other side of I-10. Do you like a well-sculpted hedge and silver SUV's? They make me nuts. I get wild punched in the arm by a Tohono O'odham nurse in eggplant scrubs. I know. It's complicated. Do you throw out your underwear every six months? *'Billy Jean'* is playing at the vaccine table under a red gazebo. Wind blows the syringe out of T.O. nurse's hand. It lands on the sidewalk. A fat dude on a bike picks it up and says his belly is too big for skinny tires. Says his pedals are trying to kill him. I ride down the Santa Cruz riverbed smashing pumpkins like a coyote with mange. Un-furred and desperate to love you again.

Nope. Can't do it. Have you read *'Chinatown'*? Do you know anything about plot, character and structure? What is your problem? How did I ever take you on as a client? I haven't liked one word you've written in thirteen years. You're a hack. A charlatan. A no-talent, two-bit actor trying to claw your way into the writing biz. I have standards. Artistic standards for intellectual property. I have a super successful, mega-hot wife who sucks my balls at the end of the day. Do you know what her net worth is? I don't need this! Fuck your stupid screenplay. I don't give a shit. Hey, if you wanna talk more about this, call me. Alright, if you want to sign a non-discloser, call me. Okay?

Is this emotional puke fest making you sick? You always hated when I was preoccupied. I should get drunk and sodomize some chick. I wonder what you miss. Do you miss French fries? Or my plaid Paul Bunyan shirt? If I were dead I would miss stupid things. Like the sign in front of the laundromat. Parking lots, strip malls, gas stations, bull dogs. I would miss girls in low-slung jeans with pink eyeshadow and tats. Or crushing on Tennessee stud Forrest. Public vertical sex at El Parador. I would miss open windows. Night breezes. Velvet stars. Stray cats. Sirens. Early morning, male gambel quail calls. Lay it on me man.

Do you ever hear men talking? And don't know if they're speaking to their wife or a dog? Chrissy Tieg just cancelled her Twitter account. See you're not missing anything. A girl in my writing class self-identifies as a 'queer crip.' Once she held up a red magic marker drawing of every pain spot in her body. It was the best poem. Why do we hurt? Did I mention my ex is a direct descendent of Christopher Columbus? It's a boner-killer right? Her ancestors were beheaded in the plaza in Santa Fe. Her new girlfriend Dolly lives in Tesuque. Like Miss Parton and *'Hello Dolly'*. Who names their kid *that*?

I went to a bereavement group once in the basement of Grace Saint Paul Church. We were assigned to reflect on forgiveness. All I did was fill my notebook with lists of unforgivable acts and people. Don't tell yourself time heals all wounds. Don't talk to the wrong people about your pain. Feel the hole inside you. Don't outgrow your need for revenge. *Chingasos* galore! I hope that gold-digger, Barbie cunt Melania Trump is hog-tied and dragged back to Slovenia.

I'm hooked on *'American Idol'*. It's tacky. And turns the human voice into a commodified spectacle. Hey, I'm into it. I'm scrounging for distractions. Last night, two girls belt *'Grenade'* by Bruno Mars in a sick duet. I watched it ten times and wept. Then I had a bad dream Covid Baby is shanking homeless dudes behind the church dumpster. She's listening to Taylor Swift, wearing a Juicy Couture, rhinestone collar and hiding in a crack in the wall. I saw her hacking out a pigeon's heart with a machete. Should I call 911? Perfection is lame. I mean even Anne Sexton was a creepy predator.

Is there any point in re-creating the chaos, intensity and immediacy of World War II? Why do people keep telling Polish jokes if they're not racist? Dumbass Polacks. Did you know it's allegedly legal to eat your Chia pet? Kristi says everyone in Arkansas fucks their first cousin. Do you believe what people say? Have you been to the Hooters on Broadway? Why is their mascot an owl with huge, orange, implant eyeballs? I don't get it.

I cut you off when mom was dying. She was a take-no-prisoners, platinum goddess who boiled potatoes, scrubbed floors and smacked your *dupa*. We sang *'Sto Lat'* on her deathbed. Her hair blew up side-ways like Mr. Magoo. She smelled like thistles. She wore a glitter maxi dress and Jackie O sunglasses on the last day. I was crying. Sitting in the Vegas airport staring at a Latino homeboy. Playing video poker on an *'Orange is the New Black'* machine. Crazy Eyes gaping at me like a plexi-glass, gambling addict. Why didn't you tell me about the cancer? My grandmother died of a cancerous brain tumor. Dad put her bed in the dining room so she could see the tulip magnolia and count the birds.

Aguska told me you're married. She and I are leaving Polish class at the U.A. discussing the Polish axe dance. *'My friend Zigor knows it.'* *'Oh, you know Zigor? You must know his wife and three kids?'* It's February, 2017 and *mamushka* is dying. I knew you were a player. But this is a total head banger. You never return my emails.

So I call your wife. It's like talking to a Margaret Atwood character. You know, Stepfordian. I say *'I'm not the keeper of sexual secrets.'* Slavic Mail Order Bride says I'm a lunatic. That you are her alarming prince charming. She thinks I'm making all of this up. I apologize and say I would never have slept with you if I would have known. You and I don't speak. Then you got brain cancer and Covid and died. Hey, the male giraffe is not monogamous either. Just for the record, I'm not into giraffe vaginas. No biggy. You jacked up artifact. I'm so over this.

Wild cucumber vines are blooming under the mesquite. Their spike bombs look like the spiteful virus. Covid Baby is riled up. She thinks she has the same DNA as Rihanna. She's dropping rufies in communion wine. Yelling get down girl. She's massacring all the dreamers. I saw her put the Easter Bunny in a chokehold. She slammed his groin and is spitting sour milk in his face. That bitch needs to quit looking at me like I'm *loco*. She laced Neopolitan, white chocolate truffles with razor blades. Always snooking around. I'm onto her. Have you ever stepped into Satan's shoes?

Our unborn child speaks 2,649 pornographic languages. Hold your dream softly she screams. Her most deviant act is incubating a dead animal. Playing dress up. To hostile memories. And atrophy of desire. This is the winter of skin, bones and teeth. This is the summer of luxury thugs. The child says she will break your ugly neck. If you write a declaration of love. The child says I will sing a crude oratorio. She's taking snapshots of photoluminescent shame. Of voluptuous loneliness. Of the eulogy I haven't written yet. Of the requiem I have not played. What voices does the body hold? Are you cool, silky menace and hyper-charismatic? I'm glaring at the cibachromes of your icky, incandescent corpse.

I went to Ace Hardware this morning to buy air filters. This is Holy Week. Haven't we suffered enough? Full-time contractors at Ace are playing with wind-up baby chicks for $3.99. Weird Cougar in a Bar pulls up in her lime green, Lamborghini Aventador. She's got peyote and *mezcal* from Teotitlan del Valle. She wants to trip and heal your wounds. To make everything right. Covid Baby's a beast. She's giving free, bomb head to Hassidic Jews on their way to the synagogue.

How did I create a scenario that you got to hurt me? Did I hurt myself? Am I full of blame and holding a grudge? Remember when trannies still had their dicks? Remember poppin' wheelies, dental dams and trojans with nonoxynol. What the hell's in spermicide anyway? What are you wearing? I like the old Italian tux with a cummerbund. Field corn. Vermillion flycatchers. A thousand ripe tangerines. An onstage crucible. Muscular forearms. Unphotogenic moments of negotiating sexual power. A Serbian tango. A Oaxacan night club pumping *la banda*. Are you sure you weren't fried and wasted?

Last summer, I had an iridescent lizard trapped in my house. I think it was the spirit of Federico Garcia Lorca. She/he lived underneath a plastic, tupperware container I use to store lasagna. Jammed behind my NPR fifteen-foot desk. Lizard shit is white. Did you know that? They can live ten days without food or water. I happen to live in a land of 559 lizards. Do you recall descending into Neoproterozoic time? Into the dream where the wicked king went up in smoke.

Slavic Mail Order Bride has an abortion. Three months after I call her and tell her you're a piece of split-lipped, back-stabbing, man candy. It's snowing. There's an elevator shaft in my heart. You state publicly you're unhappy with the pregnancy. Since you already have three grown children. This blows. Weird Cougar in a Bar laments. He was inside my house. And inside my body. Who is this guy? There are so many of us. We got rizzed. An entire plush, female, spatch-cocked body choir. My eyes can't stop rolling. People are so petty.

All the sociopaths lying back in Lazy Boy recliners in their parent's basements are now on a shooting spree. As soon as the pandemic leveled off, they went to Walmart and bought semi-automatic weapons. You were at our office today. Discussing male violence. Showing us some insurance options. Covid Baby is heavy-lifting at the gym. She just shared a naked Instagram selfie. A nine-year old in Minneapolis takes the witness stand. Can I talk to you in private?

In December, you will be ice-skating in a bright, crocheted, orange scarf. The trees will speak to you. I will make hot cider and apple cobbler. You will twirl and fall. I will carve a hole in the ice. That will spew body parts. Chewed up legs and feet. Don't be afraid. Pick up each random hand or mouth or eyeball. Pray for mercy. Love the amputated heart. Praise each ventricle. Stitch them into a necklace of limbs. Remember who I am. Love the grimy, fleshy tongue and rotten teeth. Memorize her. Surround her with stars.

I'm lusting after the Whole Foods cashier. He's half my age giving me boner jams. So what. My heart is not a bruised nectarine. I'm not a little man with a magenta hairdryer inside the freezer with a secret password or cello arpeggio. I am not slowly searching. For more hyped up analysis. For non-existent notes or a white rabbit, statue of St. Joseph or embroidered, red rose on a Krakow cross. I'm not a glam photo of mom at the beach. I'm not the unmailed letter or the tinted, vanquisher goggles. The *guapito* baby screaming selfie is not me. I am not an archipelago of glitzy lips and octopi. I am a swaggy voyeur welded inside the chambers of your heart.

Don't consult the I-Ching. Or gaze lovingly at my letter opener. I am not the hand holding the pen. Or the apicoectomy. I am not the hair in the drain. I'm not the high priestess with a hard-on eating old sushi. I am the ultra-magnification of the first movement. I do have unencumbered time to reflect. I'm not a closeted bisexual in a motel room with his pants down. I'm not a container of shame. Or sad compendium of all my unwritten work. I am not wild. Nor suicidal or burning or worshipping the sun that looks like a moon. I am not the vast wash of sound falling away. I am your dime piece ejaculating infinite nodes of destiny.

Your dick looks like a portobello mushroom. Sometimes. Not always. Not in a good way. Usually when you were wasted. I don't give a shit. Take exquisite care of what you can. Don't try to control anything. Don't watch the clock. Take ten deep breaths. Don't breathe at all. Why are you asking me? Rub arnica on at night. Hold someone's hand. Reminisce about pre-Covid times. When I was with my father. I could hold Opal. I could sing to a baby. I slept well. I ran through airports. I didn't shake at night. I dressed up. I stood close to strangers. I touched people I didn't know. I did the psychedelic *cumbia* with sleazy *salseros*. I didn't worry I was going to die. You were still here.

Language is a trampoline. Is there nothing more scintillating than the long, human history of verbal insults and slurs? You reek. Schizophrenia runs in your family. Two toddlers are smuggled and dropped from a fourteen-foot border wall. Four men are arrested for gang-raping a Bengal monitor lizard. Where do you go when you get scared? Shame on you brat. They don't serve ghettos spreads in hell. I lost my appetite. Can we go to Sky Zone and dive into a moshpit of day-glo yellow sponges?

I don't admire anyone who watches re-runs of 'Love Boat'. Did you know you can buy Jew emoji's on the App store? A little, ultra-Orthodox *brujo* goes a long way. Do you wanna go to the mustard museum and share a soft, sesame pretzel? Can't we just turn off the lights and bliss out? You were always jealous of my hermaphrodite girlfriend. Which is crazy because it was a long time ago. She was all clutch and next level chaos. A drop-dead, gorgeous, raw, copper butch. We met at St. Hilda's gym in Harlem. She ate like a vulture. A dope fiend. She cooked pot roast in the Bronx and her crank smelled like gold. She was a carnival ride gone haywire. A dangerous toy. Are you sly, insatiable and extinct? I feel like I'm not really needed here. I'm hitting the mute.

I was blamed for the Thirty Years War. An object of scorn and cruel scrutiny. Guilty of witchcraft and adultery. My hair contains chronic, gold, blown glass. I was forced to walk barefoot carrying a dead owl. They put laxatives in the meat. Family dinners were awkward. Our marriage was morganatic, unwritten and unconstitutional. Why on god's green earth would you leave? I never thought you would die. I'm accused of love, friendship and the worst of all—female virility and the tyranny of time.

You don't belong to me. You never did. Is your origin story a killer podcast? I'm a big fan of classical-style, stage combat and fist fights. Fifth brain interludes. Parallel and paradoxical narratives. Can you fill the attic with 1,267 suitcases and saints? I think that's about bad mentorship. All I want is a sequin, paisley, mini dress that shimmers. Kiss me. Be kind gentle doom. Hell is so near and far away. Stain the world with suns. My ultimate, fantasy breakup is here.

Masked bandits are spying on me. Degrading my windows. Someone taped a note to my door. You need to show me how bad you want it. Or do you just want to fuck and go back to the trailer park? I have smelly rags all over. Someone is laying on top of me trying to smother me. I'm slamming the side door shut. It won't close or lock. I keep trying to jam it. There are people living in the building on the other side. One grief leads to the next. Where were you when *matka* died?

I'm stranded in an airport. Pennies and pocket change sprawl over a large table. There are women who know me. Smart. Fashionable. Witty. I'm wearing a hat. A *spodik*. I'm so frustrated. I'm missing my flight. The subway platform is packed with sailboats and then it's empty. I walk past a very modern, outdoor mobile sculpture. Are you stuck? Keep spithalling. Keep counting the piles of tears. Keep counting on comfort. Are you waiting for something that's already gone? Solitude is not failure. Are you blooming in broad daylight?

Brazilian women can watch porn and whack off at work. I am on the verge of a scientific and magical breakthrough. I am randomly bursting. I fell in love with a man who sold his skin. I swallowed something whole. The furnace. An armadillo. A gangrene arm. When the world was ending, you left me. Latex vinyl stretched tightly over your janky mouth. I'd rather be optimistic and extroverted like Bach.

I am a girl soaked in a jar. A hemorrhaging nerve. Picking out shards of bone. Can the dead dis each other? I mean almost everyone knows you were a major disappointment. Death is greedy. Should I take an eight-week course on *'Talking to Dead People'*? A woman in Bristol had sex with 159 ghosts. It was covered by the BBC. Are you in a world that exists beyond the human mind? How can I unpack that?

It's Good Friday. I'm meditating on the agony in the garden. And the poor man's blood sausage. If anyone's dick got near *babcia's* stove, it could be mistaken for *kieshka*. Chopped up. Fried and eaten. Or sold with a hundred pounds of smoked *kielbasa*. I'm binging Season 3 of *'Shtisel'*. It's an Israeli, understated, soap opera shot in Jerusalem in Yiddish. Michael Aloni is the hottest Hassid on hunk-o-pedia. I love the close up of cheesecake. I'm really sick of this wreckage and aftermath. This is one of those times. It will be over soon. I wish I could polka with you.

I don't like being female. I'll tell you a secret. I'm not a de-fetishized virtual zoo. Passion is always political. When did this room get so small? I have to write a *zuihitsu* for class. I'm growing my Rumpelstiltskin beard out. Brilliant white, long imp whiskers. The one thing I was dreading is a slurpee. I think I'm totally an old soul. Holy shit, yes we get to jitterbug. By the way, why does baby jesus look just like that nutjob Kyle Rittenhouse?

I remember you scrubbing me like a raw potato. You pulled my ears and scoured my neck like a dejected, 19th century eastern European orphan. I'm not a valentine radish. Or lifesize, stuffed, taxidermy squirrel. You loved when I made mistakes. I'm an olive green, doom-scrolling monster in a hospital. Writing the celibate slut manifesto. No water lilies or somber, funeral march of Frederic Chopin. *'Ciotka you have to eat!'* Just a quiet, undignified death.

Why do my hetero besties give me trendy, queer bestsellers? Seriously. Do they think I need to read about who I am? Who are these benevolent, pansy rednecks? Why does everyone think they're a curator of queerness? I have a serious case of snow vertigo. I'm snipping arms off ugliness. The sky is a red dress with exposed seams and zippers. Where are you, dark hole of love? Give yourself kisses everywhere it hurts. I'm glue-gunning our fingers together. So they never pull apart. I'm lighting candles and reciting novenas. No one needs to know any of this.

I want Frankie Yankovic to sing *'Who Stole the Keishka?'* at my grave. I saw a snapshot of the afterlife. A stock agency photo. A tired man with a coffee cup. A few gutterpunk angels, blue heron and a deformed Venus. God is caught with embarrassing content on his laptop. He's wearing silk pajamas and a fedora. Do not ignore your flesh.

It's hard to look at this photo. Your wife's elastic smile snaps over a velvet-trimmed bodice. She's dressed like Julie Andrews in *'Sound of Music.'* Her hair slicked tight in a ponytail. You in a *kolpak*, a large, black hat with an eagle feather. And a richly-embellished, hand-stamped leather belt with an extraordinary buckle made of welded metal runes. She's wearing an embroidered blouse with puffy sleeves. Her skirt is wool to avoid the snowy, Carpathian winter. Your sons are in white pants and leather boots. Their vests are black with red embroidery and bells. Your daughter's wearing flowers in her hair. A babushka tucked into her white apron.

Covid Baby is booked on charges of indecent exposure. Weird Cougar smashed the Lamborghini and is dropping acid. Mail Order Bride installs a chain link fence with spiral, razor-barbed, concertina wire and five-hundred-pound, sand bags around your toxic ghost. She says I'm a threat to your family and all of humanity. She's obsessed with feral cats. I am burning anonymously in hell. The Basque mob is after me. I'm a widow and orphan. I quit. I can't take this. I'm making *golumpki* and goulash.

Your wife's hand is on her hip. The boys are on one knee. You stand over a fire pit twirling an axe. Your daughter is wearing eyelit, red beads, a scalloped bodice and purple floral skirt. Your sons carry a *bartka*. The man's wedding dress has a silk kerchief around the neck. Your bride dons an intricate headdress made of feathers and flowers. The groom's straw hat is covered in yarn pompons and large tassels made of grass. You all smile wide and are catching birds. A photo bomb from *National Geographic*. Your sons stomp, turn and kick, swinging the hatchet in a figure 8.

How can I tell the truth about us? *Schnitzel*. Candles. A *babka*. A cardboard crown. Don't shush me! I have no celery or animal crackers. We are in a non-ideal situation. Sharks existed before trees. Pay homage to the greasy images of my heart. Do you have a vaccine passport? Can you make moaning sounds? Here's how I see it going down. I am too skilled, deep and desperately hungry. Too tenacious on the glass. Too many gnats. You can't swat 'em all. It takes a hundred million neurons to create one thought.

Listen to me whatever your name is. I'm done. So they say. Like a donkey making potato pancakes. I've lost my mind. I'm walking humbly. Wrapping this up. Make sure you don't do anything stupid. You will always live in my scalded and vacant heart. My breathe shall determine the fate of the world. I can't tell what's left. I'm not attracted to you anymore. Not even in the least. I have an international, award-winning moustache. I want to fuck Megan Thee Stallion like the gods of war.

Can you meet me at IHOP on Grant? I'm onto you. What's it like to decompose? Underage Hooker's kicking rocks in the alley at 7:46 am Easter morning. She's in pig-tails carrying a backpack and lugging a sparkle suitcase. When I say *'hello'* she spits a pinecone necklace in my face. Do you think she made it herself? A cow fell out of a livestock trailer and was seen running. Did you know a kid found a fifty-thousand-year-old Mastodon tooth? Remember when we ate raw, wooly mammoth burgers with pickles? I believe we were beautiful.

You're getting married in three days. Love is like Christmas at Pizza Hut. It's a funny bizness. I'm smearing it all over the walls in abstract expressionist style. Everyone want to be seen. And publicly heard. Everyone wants the spot. Warhol's fifteen minutes of excruciating nose-bleeding fame. Do you want to be a chubby, trans, Calvin Klein, Times Square super model? Am I a disgusting, sloppy joe chef burying your afterbirth?

I call the hotline. One hundred and sixty-five million doses of vaccine have gone out. Hummingbirds arrive with throats like ripped roses. Where'd you go? I'm joining a billionaire club with Bukowski and Plath. Charles writes uncensored girlie action to die for. All ass and bounce. It punches back. It pulls. Unzipped and underneath. Slapping. A crenellated nymph bangs a six-cylinder smokestack bitch. A savage bog of gyrating flesh. Strangling stands of ripping moss and sadness. Rampant sunrise and yowling red hair. Misplaced. Awry. Why do feminists detest him? What's wrong with you people?

I'm not doing it. I'm not making myself smaller. Yes, I'm in love with a distorted version of you. I'm a hyper-megalomaniac Leo with the same birthday as J-Lo. How can you not listen? It creeps in. Like twat shots and spam burgers. You can't avoid stuff. Are we eating the housekeeper's *hors d'oeuvres*? Grief is burly. It will have it's way with you. Like a bridezilla hairdo dance. Sounds so jaunty. Am I responsible for your silence and the swallows in your gullet? What is that word that means to un-drown oneself? *Desahogarse?*

Cherry blossoms explode. Covid Baby tweets two ex con, female, Texas rappers. Little frickin' carnivore. She's in a striped catsuit stitched with enlarged, infected spleens. Staggering in snakeskin stiletto boots. Franz Kafka's cockroach has crawled inside my uterus. Is it a new-fangled IUD?

Columbia University has a Center for Complicated Grief. No joke. Is your pain fresh? Is it getting better? Or worse? I can feel a radiating super nova in my chest. Floating like a big-eyed, silver sardine. My teeth hang like grey, shimmering eels. Are you fast and easy? I'm dripping inside a monochromatic, baby-making machine.

I need to wrap this up. We're swapping nasty holes of gratitude. And feuding on a pre-loaded, Alexa video-chat, software app. It's all spilt milk and spectacle at this point. Suturing gouged memories. Festering illegal fireworks. This is not a reciprocal relationship. I'm running out of steam. I had a big life and a delicious ass. I fucked all the leading men. I take two hostess cupcakes and squish them into my eyes. No one notices chocolate marshmallow tears. Do you think my neighbor hears me crying at night? Why weren't we married by a rebel punk preacher? You stepped on a swan's neck. Who has swans in their fucking wedding? That's ridiculous. I just ate lunch with Robert de Niro. Whoever the hell he was.

Covid Baby is a super spreader. She's going places. This kid's on fire. She's rockin' a shy vibe trucker hat. Wrangling rodeo dudes and mutton-busting. Her new crush is a country super star in distressed, ripped Wranglers. He's soul-driven and ready for a reckless start. The spiritual realm is not a logical place. Tsunami's are scary. Weird Cougar in a Bar is getting her hands dirty. She's putting false eyelashes on with rubber cement. Trans Carpathian Widow hangs your decimated hands on the clothesline. There's never a perfect time.

I'm sitting at Dr. Migliazzo's waiting to get two cavities filled. Covid Baby crashes through the dental office lobby window like a sharp-shinned hawk. Trapezoids of glass dance across the carpet. She crawls under a chair biting and gurgling like a rabid dog. She's dragging pieces of the emergency helicopter pilot who airlifted you to the hospital. Empress mode, *mon cheri!* What an eye opener.

Morning sun, a boiled amphibian beet. The Old Pueblo is slammed with glitches, slackers and stoners. Remember when you tore an eye out of the Komodo Dragon? I didn't ask questions. Or sing. Sorrow has no voice. I don't know how long I bled. I didn't get out of the tub or reach for a towel. I'm a witness to something I will never quite understand.

I send fifty pages of this diatribe to Janklow & Nesbit. They're a prestigious literary firm on Madison Ave. The agent is from Scottsdale. His brother died of suicide and he likes Wanda Coleman. The other agent is a consummate, beyond-sexy, Casanova playboy. Like you. That's cool. He's killin' it. According to a 2013 *New York Times* article. They ran a color photo of every girlfriend or paramour. I'm having an anaphylactic reaction to this narrative. Lukewarm poetry about feelings isn't being optioned for three million.

I watch a ninety-five-year old lindy hop on Youtube. I'm trying to forget who you are. When my mother died I thought *'Is she still my mother?'* I want a bitchin' Norma Kamali, ruffle shirt circa 1980. It's only twelve bucks at Goodwill. I usually hate bell sleeves. I should write a critical essay on AIDS and COVID. But it's so depressing. You can rent a jacuzzi in the foothills by the hour and just watch the jets blast. Buck naked in a big ol' bucket of steaming water with strangers. No thanks. So rinky-dink. At least we had Grace Jones and the Clit Club. Is this a long, break-up letter?

I'm floating face down in a scummy pond of pot belly pigs and albino bull snakes. Snow is falling on flamingoes. I stare at the mica eyes of the shinagawa monkey. Is it you? Are we in a campy, zombie horror series? Look at what you do to me. If you show up here, I will escort you off the premises. You whack job. Stop it.

My heart is operatic. A bang-up, elephant circus act. A big ass attraction. I'm lashing out. I don't like sensationalizing my pain. Turning myself into a public gorgon with large teeth and wings. Weird Cougar in a Bar says you were a real head case. Hardcore narcissist. Infidelity is so old school. I mean who plays predictable, man-whore games? Haven't you heard of polyamory? What's up with all the big, little lies?

When Sophia Loren and I lived in pink sandstone Disneyland, her brother-in-law died. His ghost came through the house one night and tapped me on the shoulder. He was an alcoholic like you. Married with five kids, driving his Sedona girlfriend's SUV drunk. Next morning we drove to Navajo Mt. and watched a coyote act sketchy. He was dead but stuck in the animal world. Salone slit the neck of a sheep and squeezed out the intestines in a bucket. We picked strychnine out of peyote. His deaf brother threw up at 3:28 a.m.

On May 25, 2017, mom dies. I was in an old bath house on Green Lake watching 'Grand Concourse' by Heidi Schreck. Obsessed with the thought of her eighty-seven-year-old body being slid into the frig at the crematorium in Vegas. Death is such a bummer. Last night, I hung out with a coyote in Arroyo Chico. It stared at me for twenty-five minutes making coughing sounds. Was this you trying to tell me something? If your Chihuahua is honking, it's definitely a collapsed trachea.

Do you remember LaLa, my manic depressive boyfriend who played rubboard in black leather zydeco? He committed suicide when I was in Amsterdam. Sophia Loren called me when she heard a tribute to him on KXCI. I was pissed. Every Dutch fag with a bulldog in Vondel Park looked like LaLa.

Do you remember Samuel Martinez? A one-hundred-year-old homeless man. He was a former Pullman porter and can collector, who slept in the back of Common Grounds warehouse that stored cappuccino carts. When he died, I was driving from the emergency shelter to the ER. He was dead twenty minutes when I arrived. The nurses let me in. I touched his feet and hands. What happens to the shelterless deceased when there is no next of kin?

I've been ruminating on mitochondria. The brain chip inside my forty billion cells. And the polyethelene glycol globbing onto the outside of me. Re-incorporating into my DNA. I wonder about synergistic toxicity, protein circulation and abnormal messages. I have socks older than you.

Earth is covered in ice. You are singing Johnny Cash. We're suspended in the great angular unconformity. One-point-seven-five billion years that can't be accounted for. We're dangling in the geological gap. Purple sequin studs shimmer on the yoke of your jacket. No fish. Or shelly marine creatures. Just a sacred site of epic evolution. We wave to rafters and kayakers who waited twelve million years to get their permit. Bacteria is rampant on vertically-foliated metamorphic rock. You have vanished. Sneaky and intoxicated.

It's Sunday morning. I'm eating cheese and crackers for breakfast. I watch SNL's skit on black and white journalists covering the Derek Chauvin trial. Look up the ten-day temp forecast. Covid Baby's on Yahoo news. What a menace. She's lurching up Windsor Castle in soiled, polka dot panties, a Hazmat suit and size thirteen men's Adidas sneakers to combat the UK variant. Sucking a watermelon Eegee's and refusing interviews with the BBC. They've got a strobe on the little, squealing psycho. She's standing in for

Harry's girlfriend since Meghan Markle's pregnant and unable to travel. She's sweating, warbling a robotic text in Prince Andrew's ear. *'I'm bringing you love, so you gotta take it!'*

Gigi Gorgeous reveals she's pansexual and comes out for the fourteenth time. A Florida woman claims she's Harry Potter and fatally strikes a federal judge. What exactly is a controversial lawn ornament? My dermatologist neighbor takes an advanced open carry class. My stomach hurts. Everything feels heavy.

I should be happy. Appreciate every small thing. Instead I have low-grade dread. Who else will die? Why is Michigan off the hook? Fuckin' Midwesterners. What the hell are they doing? If you want to pack into Detroit Tiger stadium, attend church and eat pie at Marie Callender's, the death toll will mount. The dead will drift off, hanging onto helium balloons. Living through a plague is a horrific clusterfuck. Is god taking bathtub selfies? Is she making bitchy noises? So many details.

Don't even start. I'll break it down. Why were two hundred and fifty-two children murdered in Chicago last summer? What are their names? Who were their assailants? Are they being prosecuted and televised? Look it up on the Gun Violence Archive. What about the woman who was abducted, raped and killed last year while marching at a George Floyd protest. What's her name? Does anyone know? Sorry female rape is an everyday atrocity. What about the nineteen-year-old UA student who was gun-to-the-chest executed a few weeks ago in the Cherry Street parking ramp? What about the five sixteen-year-olds that killed him? Who's Cadillac were they driving?

I record the color of golfer's shirts on the Reid Park course. Tapioca, slate, cobalt, teal, rose, banana, mango, orange and geranium. The guy who drives the machine picking up thousands of balls at the driving range wears hot pink. I believe it's mandatory. Can you imagine applying for that job? I count thirteen vehicles lined up in the drive through at In-N-Out Burger. Skip past

Panda Express, Chick-fil-A, Claim Jumper and Mattress Plus. A sliced ball soars over the chain link fence, whizzes by my right eye hitting on-coming traffic on Alvernon. Can't that guy straighten out his stroke?

Sometimes I just want to be held. Why were you the last one to hold me? I'm falling into a slot canyon of scars. My stomach hurts. Should I buy a 2009 Smart Car bomb spray-painted by Kenny Scharf? The teeny bopper hooker is back. A gargoyle wasted on meth dangling off the rails with creosote painted nails. She's an escalating scourge drooling a Niagra Falls of saliva from the 2nd floor porch screaming *"I'm a dog fucker! I'm a dog fucker!"* Why does this look so degrading and normal?

This ultra-upscale, swanky hood should be called Dead Apache. But it's named after a Welsh immigrant born in Pembrokeshire, Wales in 1829. He opened a butcher shop, married an eleven-year-old and had ten children. On April 30, 1871, he armed Anglo, Mexican and Tohono O'odham perpetrators who attacked Aravaipa Apache on the upper terrace of the east bank of the San Pedro. Allegedly he did not 'participate' in the massacre. One hundred and forty-four women and children were killed, mutilated and scalped. I have a field recording in my bedroom.

You're a stud. I refuse to apologize for primal law. My uncle Hyman said chop me up with the rest of the Russian Jews. Olga emails from Warsaw. She's shooting a post-punk, psycho drama about motherhood in 1987, Poland. The protagonist is a bi-polar bohemian seeking comfort in sex, drugs and cool, unexpected things like anarchy and snow.

Slavic Mail Order Bride is chewing a javalina skull. Underage Hooker's dragging a wheelbarrow in mean yellow sequin pants. She and Covid Baby are building a solar shower with copper pipe and bamboo. Covid Baby keeps sending me texts. *'I think about you all the time. Can't we just start over?'* She's so deranged. I'm starting to choke. A Minnesota cop pulls her gun instead of a taser. How do you do that? I will send to you a picture and phone number. I will prove it. I'm real.

Former *Bachelor* hunk Colton Underwood already has a new reality show Netflix deal. Didn't he just come out six seconds ago? No surprise. He's cashing in on queer-ness. *Hollywood Reporter* runs an expose on mega-producer Scott Rudin for throwing a tea cup, Apple monitor, glass bowl, stapler and a baked potato at his staff. He also called his theatre assistant 'a retard'. '*To Kill A Mockingbird*' brought in 1.5 million a week. Scott's going nowhere. He has unimpeachable taste and lofty literary ambition. I mean he didn't rape or murder anyone. And Cuomo. First off he's Italian. And who hasn't been hit on by their boss?

Sunrise. Butterflies lick eucalyptus bark. Children rip bullets into children. Whites are shooting blacks. Blacks are taking out Asians. The bougainvillea is busting magenta Japanese paper kites. My eyes aren't matching. Titus' saliva swims in a tube. That gets shoved into a metal box that goes to a lab at NYU that sends a text to his iPhone app that says positive or negative which allows him to get on the Staten Island ferry and show Bong Joon-ho movies in a locked classroom where he's five-hundred-feet away from each international film student.

Let us go, you and I, when evening spreads, a cauterized mermaid in the sky. I'm a venus sex kitten in lavender, Italian boots. Moving softly beneath clouds, scratching a gill with my hind leg. Hair curled, rings of champagne and smoke around olive green eyes. My red sequin scales flayed with blood stains and civilized lives. I'm an aquatic critter with no body. My head crawling around the bottom of a tank. My face ruffled and heart falling through a trap.

This is a story of bones. The mushrooms my *dziadek* ate. An unknown village in Northeast Poland. A baby born without a tongue. A man who studies human landslides. I never knew why *buscia* named my mother after

Saint Petronilla. A woman lying in a coffin with flowers in her hair and a broom, awaiting the newly dead into heaven. I believe the story to be holy. I understood persecution. Saint Petronilla swills a blade to my mother's throat. We're sitting in a black, Plymouth station wagon ready to buy root beer in mid-July. *Tra-la-la*. It's like watching an eclipse. Or an extended, quiet, primal scream. The first time I see random evil in bright green sunlight.

Are you stalking me? Are you compressed into a tiny, plexiglass box adjusting your breathing and heartbeat? Are you a contortionist in shock? How did you get here? How did this happen? I see you folding up your life into a prehistoric origami of time. Are you trapped in a giant, scrotum-shaped glass? One grain of wedding rice never thrown dropping on your head. I have scraped light off the eastern sun. Have you been ravished and licked by god?

My landlady wants to raise the rent $75 dollars. Staszek wants to make a movie with Sophia Loren and Chiwetel Ejiofor. We've exchanged 143 emails. I have a blistering fantasy about Stasz being my Polish producer boyfriend. I don't think he's interested. I mean we haven't even met. He just read my script *Blood Soup* which is way more intimate than sex. I've already thought about my dress for Cannes. A red, sheer chandelier unlocking a gang buster vault of human bile.

I'm in hyped overdrive. I have another dream where you're telling me about a *menage* you had with two porno babes. You're all cranked up. I'm trying to find privacy and put on make-up. How does the body gestate grief? Let's just get into it. Is it a necrophiliac, lounge singer vibe? Is it night winds sweeping over metallic coils? Is it like last week's Fed Ex mass shooting televised on CNN? Is it like eating too many Lorna Doones and Altoids? Is it like circumambulating 'Yeehaw' tatted on Ireland Baldwin's butt?

Is there anything undignified going on? What happens to your foreskin? Do you feel like an erotic cripple? I'm laying in bed listening to the sound of the train. Can you do a pantomime of the journey of the soul? Can we dance like two old, Dutch marionettes? Can you build an impermanent, paper bridge out of empty sugar packets for my shipwrecked heart? I'm counting the moments of kamikaze joy.

I'm looking at your oxfords in the shoe bin. I run my hands over your Basque shirts and suits. I look at the empty chair you sat on. Are you human? Or a miraculous, incurable, pig-faced curse. I'm falling into a bowl of otters. This is the oddly-lit, thrusting videography of a mad woman craving more sensation. A cinematic flipbook. Frowning. Sinking. My tenderness growing like gardenias in angst. Suddenly you look like an orange orangutan and I want to be near you.

Satan is a lesbian. Her biggest problem is the yellow-throated marten. It pisses on it's tail and shoves beehives off their perches. I am running along the Santa Cruz and stop at the only bathroom. A concrete block used by river rats and homeless folk. An unshaven dude comes out and gets on his bike. I go in and gaze at the metal bowl filled with this guy's floating crap. Does the poop of strangers bother you?

After being quarantined and socially-deprived, I bust out of the house. And head to Zona Libre to meet a recent, fullback recruit for U.A. Wildcats. I'm wearing a blingy, bodycon dress and sheer, Botticelli, birth-of-venus crop top. Tony's Haitian and Dominican and moves like an underwater, voodoo matador. We convert tons of pandemic anxiety into a sliced *bachata* by Daddy Yankee. Cece, the club's Cardi B is a pulsing mosaic of implants, fake eyelashes and rippling, fuchsia hair. She's gyrating over little Raul in a free, lewd, public lap dance. Sexy *payaso!* Heaven is empty. *Los diablos estamos aqui.*

Gwyneth Scally's paintings hang in the lobby. Oil tableaux of mermaid henchmen and Goldilock's grandmother. You and I sit outside because it's windy and just rained. There's dust everywhere. Our waiter is Japanese and talks about the double rainbow. I thought he said *'stubborn rainbow.'* Which

I really like the sound of. I'm wearing velvet pants and my hair is stuck with bobby pins of sepia tone images of people touching. A man swimming with an elephant. A duet of somersaults. We're surrounded by cheetahs and sand dunes. Old architecture. We live close to the tides. And connect with animals. A woman is flailing her arms like the wings of a bird. Giant grasshoppers. Lemurs. The spider.

I was the last person to get called. So I'm in a weird head space. Obsessed with the cobwebby, badly-trampled noise of social media. I'm tripping through divebars staring at the frozen face of Durga. You're crashing in my backyard. A Disneyland for recovering fuck boys. I just dressed the supernumeraries for '*Aida*'. Full orchestra, four greyhounds, a python and two camels. The music hall is no place for a baby camel.

I watch death leaking ornate orgasms. What a grifter. Is my leopard skin ruining your cardiovascular system? Fractured, back-ass argonaut got knocked up. The male's hectocotylus oscillating inside of her. This is not a nonfiction book for the Christian market. The nautilus is actually an octopus with paper-thin, multiple bodies. Sexually-dimorphic females are six hundred times heavier than the male. They secrete a thin, calcite shell and incubate 170,000 eggs until they hatch. Even Jules Verne knew that gender is a guzzling, defective veil. You eight-armed devil fish.

I'm singing you a non-surgical lullaby. A plastic poem made in China. If you're gonna tear my world apart, let's get started. Just get it done. I like my men a little toxic. I don't need to make the stage my bitch. I don't need to be chasing you. Icky with shattering regret. Lock in. Hold us the entire hypnagogic time. Do you remember the Oscar de la Renta gutterpunk coat? Tumultuous and auspicious. A fanatical disaster. Why is Underage Hooker tweaking and twirling a baton on the upstairs porch? Forget it. Covid Baby is deep. She's studying the architecture of bones.

You were never here. Hold on. We got severed. Embossed with death. I could have a conversation about war. Use glitter somewhere. Mention a horrible thing your mother did. Talk about a thousand shazams of ecstasy. Or just keep shrinking in reverie. Where does this end? Can I write a poem that slices like a knife? It looks bad on my end. A regular old webcam. Tell me you don't care. I'm digging up *pysanky* eggs.

Have you met any war orphans? Hypatia of Alexandria? Or Lady Godiva? Is heaven an aquarium of catastrophe? Stacks of human hair, decorated enamel dishes, eye glasses, brushes, cold cream jars, shoe shine wax, baby sweaters, prayer shawls, a porcelain Mickey Mouse and 43,525 pair of shoes. A two-month-old infant dying from a rat bite.

I'm on a seventy-five-pitch climb into manhood. Whatever that is. I say. Be quiet. Live in silence. Open a door. Lick the earth from your fingers. Love the butch heart. Fried with liver and onions. Here. Eat what's left. It will taste like the moon colliding with the sun. It will taste like failure. Like the hunger of belonging. It will smell like diamonds and blood.

My uncle Lloyd moo-ed like a cow. He was the only Kentucky hillbilly I knew when I rode my scarlet fire engine down the block, trampling rectangles of grass. Machete green and sharp. My mother would die 87 years later, but then she held me in heels and a pencil skirt. I scowled like an armadillo in my tight, baby bonnet. I did not want an undiagnosed skin rash on my feet. Or to get my period at a Chicago White Sox game. I wasn't even around when my parents had unscandalous sex in November, 1956. I was not born handcuffed, skeptical and rude. Provoking civil war. I am this magical thing. Un-perfumed. A genius on the vaginal floor. Kicked out into a displaced world.

When I grew up in St. Clair Shores, there was no PFLAG. Or GLYSEN. No gay-straight alliance or *Out* magazine with treatises on homoerotic etymology, queer poop, butt plugs, trans super models or Jeremy O. Harris as the unexpected, black dandy saving the theatre world. I'm a pre-Stonewall, pre-Title 9 baby. Just an ordinary, grotesque, female beast. In matador pants searching for a dictionary. Trying to love all the showgirls at the Bellagio with a blurry, red exit wound. For those of us who crawl the edge slashing love in hallways, badly-lit stairwells, live sex acts in pipe tunnels with perennial ghosts and wet laundry. We will not dream this death of ours. Survivors who didn't survive. Who are always afraid. A gouge in the forehead, bereft of moonlight. We steal. Play a mass in C minor. And when we peel off our skin. We are the ones we love.

I message ladykiller Clint, asking where you're buried. He's another rugged stuntman at Old Tucson Studios. I'm still searching for your dead body. Like a wild elephant sifting bones in the sand. Elephants grumble and throw high-pitched screams in the graveyard. Chimpanzees hold a dead social partner tight, but abandon them once the carcass starts to decompose. And a lioness will sniff. Then lick a dead male of the pride before devouring his body.

People say I look like Kim Basinger, Martha Stewart and Elon Musk's mother. I'm not into anything shoddy or amateur. There are 27 new Covid outbreaks at my dad's assisted living. What's it like to be next to a body? A twenty-one-foot room of tainted skin, a riot of moles and hangnails. Strange, little bumps on a neck. Abnormal growths. Armpit odor. Bloated gums. The heart rotating like the aperture on a Hasselblad. Re-adjusting a million time per day to accommodate the dazzling paleontologists of time.

I'm sitting in the dark in a tempest of styrofoam containers thinking about you. The dead Basque pirate pulling people over a razor's edge into another life. What a slugfest. You are the midwife dilating the cervix of this world so the killed children and extinct species and the slain students and black youth and baby-gophers-about-to-be-eaten and the un-mourned, unacknowledged, not recognized or accounted for, like my dad's best friend's wife who died of Covid alone in a hospice on Flamingo Road breathing. Then not. I have to buy socks and go to the bank.

Were you drafted? Was your number in the pimp spot? Did you walk safely with scissors in the rain or vanish spitting against the sky? Do you remember the panoply of clouds? Did you go hungry and bare-chested, smash cuts to the eyes? Were you made of stained, translucent gypsum, shaved with a sabre-tooth bit? Into shoulders that swam. A chin twitching into wings. Do you remember the boy dance? Do you remember falling asleep, breaking fences or losing money on a whim? We are taking back the quiet, bone-fleshed creatures. Not yet euthanized. Not yet decomposed with maggots and flies. Imagining a world that doesn't yet exist.

The super cute cashier at Whole Foods got his tats amped up with day-glo ink. I stare at his forearm throbbing like a muscular, portable Sistine Chapel. A kundalini riot. I'm having a total ceremonial-fire, religious experience at check out. Slavic Mail Order Bride is hanging in the parking lot immersed in a 5th century song from the Lithuanian Commonwealth. Weird Cougar is hallucinating on mushrooms at Yoga Oasis. Covid Baby's in L.A. punching out *paparazzi* sitting on Lionel Richie's lap. It's a late night audition. *'Where are you from? Why are you wandering the Dolby theatre at this hour?'* Covid Baby makes cricket sounds. Blow dries her hair. Stumbles onto the stage in a spanx and screams. She's all about dirt-piling the hardware. Lionel yells *'Give us all of you!'*

You do not need erectile performance enhancers. Keep me in your heart for awhile. For real. Humpty Dumpty. You smell musty. There's a ticking time bomb in this scene. Are you adept at assessing your own privilege? *'Today I was led by an angel into the chasms of hell. I've been there,'* wrote Polish mystic, cook, gardener, porter and nun Maria Faustina Kowalska. She took the only dress she owned to the convent. And her notebook of ecstatic visions and conversations with god. *'I send prophets wielding thunderbolts,'* said god in 1938.

I'm eating cream puffs and watching *'Lunana: A Yak in the Classroom'* on Amazon. It's shot in a remote village with child non-actors, where local people sell caterpillar fungus and cattle. The Bhutanese yak herder reminds me of you. Even though you're not from Bhutan or a yak herder. I hit pause, dash into the bathroom sobbing for thirty minutes. I'm laying like a stag stabbed with arrows bleeding on the tile floor. Saying an undisclosed prayer. Remember you are not the night. Strange witness to the bright moment of being forgotten.

Underage Hooker is moping. In her hand, she holds a fragment of the universe. I'm so over this boisterous controversy of Covid Baby colluding with the FBI. She seized Rudy Giuliani's phones and electronic devices over his dealings with the Ukraine. Now she's splitting five foot agave leaves slurping the juice. You are the shittiest swarm of mercies. We are too stunning for this world of wedding trends. I'm looking at flats in Warsaw for $25 bucks a night.

I'm often wrong about everything. I'm sitting on a heap of repressed resentment and disappointment. I try not to hope for anything. I'm watching lesbian birdwatchers flock to Berlin just to escape homophobia in Poland. That's so twisted. I'm a persecuted, ideological, rainbow pest. Not equal to normal people according to the archbishop. Where is the shifty, prayer hands emoji? I really don't care who I was. Or who we were.

I'm closing this chapter in a big way. No more tantrums party boy. Just Balkan impressionist art, cream-colored Louis XVI chairs and a Dolce & Gabbana hoodie. India is self-incinerating. An erratic, human bonfire of pyres made of black sticks covered with burnt bodies. Can I breathe in the voice of your soul? Researchers find an embalmed, pregnant mummy. With two breasts and long hair. It has no penis. Just a little foot and a small hand. Cutting the boy's hair splices into a field of dandelions. People are choking. A piece of the wall falls out. Grief is an obnoxious mouth we are forced to wear. This is such a strenuous, ostentatious relationship.

Hey *borracho,* it's my sister's birthday today. I can't dance in this girdle. Not even the jalapeno quick-step with a Mexican cowboy. Everybody knows you were all up in your feels. Wrapping up shit with a big-ass boner. I'm vibing with Staszek who has 22 Ukrainian refugees staying in his apartment in Warsaw. Are you kickin' it with anyone? Genghis Khan or Nostradamus? I won't allow anything to fester in dark corners. Slavic Mail Order Bride is downing cod liver oil. She's a wayward wind. A horse with hairy eyeballs wading through a lonesome river.

I'm the official, ball gown presser for *Hamilton's* Broadway tour. I have six gondolas on stage right for the Schuyler sisters stuffed with silk dresses the color of butter, urine, champagne and sunlight. I steam-press stage hems into an undertow of grime, angry days and hurricanes. Eliza's winter dress is like ironing turquoise waves. On break, I sit outside next to a bed of geraniums the color of 1950's vermillion lipstick. We are Covid-tested every day and masked up. I'm crushing on the bomb sniffer—a brown and white springer spaniel that licks my face. He's security and travels with the show. The bomb-sniffer's working a 12-hour shift today, matinee and evening show. Why would anyone bring a bomb to a Broadway show?

Hot garbage screen grab. How's your ankle? Are you completely recovered from da Rona? Maybe you were just partially eaten by a bear. What about everyone who went braless during lock down. Now what? Which was worse? The virus or the break-up? Covid Baby is yanking feathers out of the most instagrammable bird. It's all glamour and pizzaz. She's moonlighting as an escort for people who feel dislodged in their own skin. A binge-worthy goldmine. Non-speaking, austistic sex workers, long-haired linebackers and Marcin Dorocinski. You owe me.

You can't breathe on Christmas Eve. Paramedics rush you into an air ambulance. Covid Baby's hanging in the cockpit. Looking like a Swedish snack. Bored, distracted and twisted. She's wearing a surgically-removed bladder, heavy indigo mascara and sheer, expensive Italian stockings. She spits at you and licks your face. *'Baby, get down on it!'* Her mouth crawls like a tarantula over your junk. You pull her down and take her candy ass. She rearranges your DNA and the emotional tableau of your body. She's humming a sad Venezuelan waltz.

You're a total drama queen. Most people die quietly. You are emergency-airlifted, asphyxiating internally from hypoxic injury due to a lethal virus during a catastrophic, global pandemic on Christmas Eve. You are fat as fuck. *'I am not dead yet. I am hard to kill,'* you once declared. Airspace regulations determine a flying altitude of 4,587 feet or $268 dollars per mile or $45,000 for a delightful ride through the troposphere. Is the co-pilot an asteroid goddess? Is she sweaty and spreading hot twinkies on a euphoric beach?

I'm witnessing a brutal slaughter in Eastern Europe on my Toshiba laptop. Weapons that vaporize human bodies. Children with their legs blown off. Babies with faces smeared to train windows. Old women bleeding and crying running through bombed buildings. The U.S. 82nd Airborne is training with Polish troops in Nowa Beda. Who are all these billionaire, Russian oligarch, super-sheisty scumbags having a fire sale of their high-end real estate in London and Italy? Vladimir Putin is a ghastly, shit-faced demon thinly disguised as an ordinary man.

The EMT panics and can't resuscitate you. The world splits open. They lose your heartbeat. Fifteen seconds later you're at the portal. Dangling off a human chandelier of dead bodies and sinister sounds. Lost in high tide swept by cardiologists, skinwalkers, fire throwers, meteors, lightning, a beheaded giantess, spinning cyber ninjas, a slew of goldfinches and sobbing. Do you know where you're going? God is barfing on an old mattress. Waiting. You are DOA at Banner Medical ER.

I'm hiding in a volcanic cave to avoid the apocalypse. Your venom is pacifying me. And this molting arachnid carcass shedding it's exoskeleton. Emperor scorpions are viviparous. They hunt at night. Eat their prey alive. I'm giving birth to 227 ivory white babies. Feeding them cicadas and small mice. You stung my softest body part. Your 400 million year old jizz blasting out of your heart into ultraviolet light. I feel death pull from the soft stomach of the world, your honey-soaked hands.

Covid Baby got you. Your spirit jolts inside an echo chamber. The news punches us in the face. Reverberates through a wave of mushroom pickers, acupuncturists, shiatsu practitioners, samba instructors, yogis who drank toasted rice green tea with you, Polish folk dancers, Old Tucson gunslingers and stuntmen who demand a theatrical facsimile of Old West bro-mance with shotguns, leather chaps and whips. Luminous waifs, rotating hot fem sub fuck dolls and haphazard hook-ups wail on the public domain Facebook wall. *Did you hear Zigor died? Poor Zigor.*

I make a Slavic headpiece for *Dia de los Muertos* from giant silk peonies. I need to carry my low-budget heart in the street. See the scorched earth faces of who I live with in this dusty corner of nowhere. Little kids throw day-glo pieces of plastic into the night. *Abuetlitas* on folding chairs hold huge, grainy photos of their parent's wedding day. Jesus freaks on megaphones accuse dry river anarchists and pageant choreographers of witchcraft. Girls with pink hair bop under umbrellas of light. Stiltwalkers in polka dots and red sequin catsuits parachute in. After walking eight miles, I eat a mesquite-smoked brat and scrawl your name in pale green chalk on a wall erected for the dead.

I fed ex a baby quilt to Warsaw. Malgorzata Bela, a Polish actress starring in Netflix *'Cracow Monsters'* is hosting a young Ukrainian mother about to give birth. I lay out the Civil War tumbler with pieces of my mother's floral pajamas and hand-made binding. There are three million refugees in Poland. I think about Alexander Litvinenko's grave in Highgate Cemetery. He's buried in a radiation-proof, lead casket covered with climbing wild garlic. A reminder of the evil that sits in the Kremlin.

A chain of whispers and gasps. No one's invited to the memorial. There is no burial. We, the degenerates, freaks, silk acrobats and holy people of the aftermath fumble through our lives trying to imagine how you—Herculean, muscular, inviolate, a Goliath—could die. A massive, city-wide scavenger hunt begins. Everyone searches for a piece of you. When a giant redwood falls, the earth lets out a horrible shudder. The dust and smoke don't settle.

You crazy Zigor, the skateboarder skidding out at 175 miles an hour. You, the martial artist and choreographer. A healer who carried me in his arms like a giant bird offering a nest to a small child. You, the nomad, fortune teller, shoesmith, horse dealer, beggar and sometimes emotional thief. You, the quietly-married man with the Von Trapp family singers. You, world traveler and major player executing highly-detailed, graphic sex acts. Taking the red eye to death. Now trapped in a boneless pantomime.

I file a formal report with Chris Magnus, Tucson's chief of police against my neighbor Joey as a potential sex trafficker. I get a call from Sgt. Jacques Spronken and estimate hundreds of Latina, Native and Central American girls are on foot, without keys, strung out and addicted, some non-English-speaking going through his 2nd floor apartment. I also contact Southern Arizona Center Against Sexual Assault and SAATURN. Spronken shows up the next day at 7 a.m. with another officer banging on the predator's door. They have a 'frank discussion'. A man-to-man conversation which the detective can't legally disclose to me.

Lt. James Brady assembles an undercover surveillance unit to investigate the 'activities' but fails to gain evidence to press criminal charges. The riptide of teenage girls surges. I call the Pima County Assessor's office for the property owner's name. She lives in Connecticut, teaches abstract art at a prestigious, liberal arts college and accuses me of harassment and slander. Hey, a fifty-year-old white guy with a silver pick-up, wad of cash and a hard-on can basically do whatever the fuck he wants. No one seems to notice the fornicating, scraped girls hurdling gates in the alley staring like caged animals in an urban zoo. East Coast landowner just wants her rent money. She doesn't care about potential, human rights violations. *Bitch there are Jeffrey Epsteins everywhere.*

On January 15, stragglers from Providence gather at El Tiradito. The only Catholic shrine dedicated to a sinner buried on unconsecrated ground. It is said a young Mexican sheep rancher died here fighting for the love of a woman. An i-Phone blasts a small, smirking version of your face. A green Saint Joseph and child yellow candle flutters. Red incense burns. Leaves sway in dirt through ribbons of light and burnt wax shadows

I'm wearing silver lipstick in a strange land. You're in a prison with access to vast, streaming art-nouveau light. In a small room, I strain to kiss you through a fat slab of glass. You open your mouth and try to bite my neck like Dracula in a midnight, underground horror flick. I see that you're happy and can see the inter-connectedness of all things. Premonitions are weird.

My neighbor shoves the real Covid Baby into my arms. I stare at her blue bird, porcelain eyes. She's been catching falling stars. Staring at me like a dusty crack queen. She whispers in my ear, *'What about Paris you ratbag!'* It's a full snatch. She's aloof because she knows I always wanted an extremely flawed, delinquent male. There is no such thing as a definitive moment. Did you take a wretched piece of me with you? Is that your animal-man-slash sex machine?

I crunch Mountain Dew and Tecate cans, tibetan prayers flags, Hershey candy wrappers and multi-colored condoms around your postage stamp screen stankface. Drifters and desperadoes walk hundreds of miles to slowly scrutinize the sacred artifact. It's like the miraculous statue of Our Lord Esquipulas. Jailbirds and supernatural beings kneel. You are now floating. An inflatable Bullwinkle in the Macy's Day Parade. Untethered to earth. Off the rails and steel wheels. Over potholes and cracks in the asphalt. The pilgrims worship you with awe. Genuflecting in fanatical gratitude.

My dad is dying in a mustard-colored room 2,179 miles away. My sister will dream his skeleton is laying in the hospital bed and his spirit has already left. My mother's ghost will sit on his bed and watch t.v. His Duke University urology report indicates a softball-size tumor lodged between his left kidney and prostate. On the phone we discuss how much longer he has to live. We're waiting for the results on three biopsies. He's going to *'Shanghai Dumpling'* for Chinese food with my sister, refusing all treatment and watching the final nailbiter between the Jayhawks and Tarheels.

I'm sick of writing. There are so many things in this world more beautiful than you. A glacial ice crevasse. A *mazurka*. A cinnamon, walnut *babka* my sister made. Photosynthesis. The Mariana Trench. The thai silk, backless, halter wedding dress and french lace coat I made for Daniella. All of my grandfather's chisels. *Paczki* stuffed with forest fruit. *Kapusta*. Woodpeckers. Scarlet tanagers. Marbled lilac amaryllis. Lena Waithe in Season 3, *Master of None*. Anything my ninety-one-year-old father says. Clouds on a windy day. Strawberry rhubarb pie. Beetles. Old, cajun fiddle songs. Marmots. Rust. My day-glo orange, body glove rash guard. Agave leaves. Unpruned bougainvillea. Werewolves and dwarves. The Cyrillic alphabet. Night-blooming cereus. Sharon Stone as Ginger McKenna in *Casino*. A bright pink, feathered, partly bald-headed, spoonbill crane. Jean Michel-Basquiat painting a skull. A brass marching band. A super flower, blood moon, lunar eclipse.

You are everywhere and nowhere. I fill your pockets with falling snow. I'm a stray cat in a storm. Vivid, furious, incessant. In a ditch. Waxing. Demeaning. Rude. Blurry. Morbid. I tell you stories with my hands about swimming in a bottomless, blue lake. Trying to escape desire and trivial thoughts. I'm languishing with maggots, hunger and madness. You are everything I cannot hold onto. Frightened and fleeing. Who came from nowhere. Gone. Returning to vascular dust.

I chat with an Ob-Gyn who spent her entire medical residency in Phoenix delivering infants of sex-trafficked, ten and eleven-year old girls from Guatemala and Central America. She explains how their hips aren't wide enough to give birth along with multiple other challenges. Tonight I walk past the local, non-profit theatre where an accused statutory rapist is associate artistic director. He's adapting Kate Chopin's 19th century, feminist, short stories for stage. Does any of this bother anyone?

Yellow is so annoying. Maybe not for broken blood vessels. Did you see Lucas Hnath's play? His mother sits in a dismal motel room recounting abduction and sexual assault. The actress is shape-shifting. Mouthing words that are played on an audio recording. That's how I feel writing this. An adversarial, trashy ventriloquist opening and shutting her jaw. Tomorrow Covid Baby moves to Ohio.

I'm carrying you in a wooden box. Before you were born a dustbowl child, embedded in a dark sky. I dragged you through blue salt, ancient wars, stalactites, shipwrecked coffins and sad feathers. We evaded barbarians. You spoke with plants small enough to breathe symbols into life. I held you in my palm. A tiny, bright yellow, male American goldfinch. I weep at the beauty of your moonstone eyes. Blinking like slaughtered butterflies. Like two shimmery moths. We are nothing hiding inside a carcass of night. Trying to remember who we used to be.

Underage Hooker is hurling a suitcase. A backpack, stuffed plastic garbage bags and make-up fly off the second floor porch. It's Wednesday, 1:38 pm. At first I think she must be spring cleaning. She's bent over in a turquoise tank top, head band and tight jeans. Picking up rocks in the driveway. Or spilt jewelry. A burgundy El Camino pulls up. The trunk pops and she throws everything in. As she climbs into the back seat, a dude with a backwards baseball cap and shades slams the door shouting *'You fucking moron!'*

I stare at a small stack of stones she leaves behind in the drive and realize these letters are megalithic. They are my cairn. What I'm leaving behind to mark the love wound. A mini Stonehenge. An inflamed organ. A sad oasis of rage and wild things. No mortar. A ferocious and prehistoric burial monument. I feel your cock roaming. Like a rotting animal still inside of me. I am here. Once so were you.

Barbara Seyda is a queer, Polish-American playwright and screenwriter. She has a B.S. from the University of Wisconsin-Madison and M.F.A. from Rutgers University, Mason Gross School of Art. Seyda began writing as a journalist for *'Outweek'* in New York City in the mid-1980s. As a member of ACT UP and Queer Nation she used photography, site-specific performance, civil disobedience, critical discourse, public protest and writing as a response to the AIDS crisis. She taught at Pratt Institute, The New School for Social Research, Rutgers University and University of Arizona Continuing Education. Her published books are *Women in Love* (Bulfinch/Little Brown) winner of a Lambda Literary Award, *Nomads of a Desert City* (University of Arizona Press) and *Celia, A Slave* (Yale University Press) winner of the Yale Drama Prize.

Currently Seyda is collaborating with female rap artist/composer Angel Haze on a new hip hop opera. She's also working with award-winning film director Olga Chajdas on a new screenplay *Blood Soup* which cross-cuts between five children in Warsaw in 1942. She lives in Tucson, on the Sonoran Desert home of the Tohono O'odham people.

www.ingramcontent.com/pod-product-compliance
Lightning Source LLC
Chambersburg PA
CBHW020342170426
43200CB00006B/478